GOD
CORNBREAD
★ ★ *and* ★ ★
ELVIS

GOD
CORNBREAD
★ ★ *and* ★ ★
ELVIS

PONDERINGS ON
ORDINARY GRACES

JOE E. PENNEL JR.

UPPER
ROOM BOOKS®
NASHVILLE

The Upper Room° website http://www.upperroom.org

UPPER ROOM°, UPPER ROOM BOOKS°, and design logos are trademarks owned by The Upper Room°, A Ministry of GBOD°, Nashville, Tennessee. All rights reserved.

Cover and interior design: Micah Kandros / www.micahkandrosdesign.com

Library of Congress Cataloging-in-Publication Data

Pennel, Joe E.
  God, cornbread, and Elvis / Joe E. Pennel Jr.
     pages cm
  ISBN 978-0-8358-1223-8 (print : alk. paper) -- ISBN 978-0-8358-1224-5 (mobi : alk. paper) -- ISBN 978-0-8358-1225-2 (epub : alk. paper)
1. Christianity--Meditations. I. Title.
  BR123.P46 2013
  242--dc23
                         2013002811

Printed in the United States of America

In memory of Mary Ann Haney—

a servant of God

and my administrative assistant for twenty-five years

★ CONTENTS

★ INTRODUCTION

In 1977 I started writing a few paragraphs for my weekly church news-letter. I made an effort to set aside time every Monday morning for this purpose. During the week I would try to take notice of life as it unfolded around me. When some person or situation would catch my attention, I would make a note on whatever piece of scratch paper I could find. These notes would inform my Monday morning writing routine.

One day a member of my congregation said, "Joe, this week's arti-cle is worth pondering." Her comment stayed with me, and the very next week I called the article "Ponderings." The title stuck, and since then, I have yet to use another.

At the urging of my wife, Janene, and my friend and colleague, Dr. Douglas N. Norfleet, I decided to select a few of these ponderings for this book.

In writing these pieces, I tried to connect to the reader by follow-ing two guidelines. First, I wanted to reflect on life from the vantage point of the Christian faith. Second, I hoped to help the reader ponder, in a much deeper way, the meaning in everyday matters.

Not all of these meditations were received positively. People dis-agreed with my opinions, and they said so. From time to time, this lack of concurrence opened the door for honest, nonjudgmental discus-sion. In every instance of opposition, I found some grain of truth that I needed to hear. That is what happens when we speak the truth in love.

I am grateful for the moving of God's spirit through the lives of friends, family, and others who inspired me to think about those ideas that are worth pondering and those that are not.

LIFE
LESSONS
★ ★

⭐ LIFE'S CHANCEL AND NARTHEX

Every Sunday morning I take a walk. After offering the benediction, I walk from the chancel to the narthex of the church. It is a short walk, but it can be exceedingly painful.

Inside the chancel rail, life is ordered and poised. Hours and hours of preparation have gone into making the service full of warmth and dignity so that God may be worshiped. It is here that the scriptures are read and the word proclaimed. The old story is told and retold. The routines at the table and font exhibit God's grace and providence. The choir leads the gathered voices of the congregation in the singing of hymns, the saying of prayers, and the recitation of psalms. God's word is shared and affirmed. Life is supported and reflected upon by the traditions of the church and the Christian faith.

But after fifty minutes have passed, I lift my arms in benediction, promising the blessing of God for the coming week. Then I go to the narthex to greet the congregants as they leave to be Christ in the world.

In the narthex, life is different. Those who have worshiped make a disorderly reentry into the world of muddled marriages, midlife boredom, adolescent confusion, ethical ambiguity, and emotional stress. In the narthex, I don't hold the cup of the Lord's Supper. Instead I shake the hand of the man whose wife has left him for another. In the narthex I do not hold the infant for the waters of baptism, but I look into the eyes of a mother whose teenaged daughter is full of rebellion. The hands that just held the scriptures now touch the hands of those who are tense with anxiety, fear, and pain.

As I stand in the narthex, I know that in the days that lie ahead there will be deaths no one expected, accidents no one thought possible, illnesses that defy diagnosis, and conflicts no one anticipated. But I also know that in the days that lie ahead there will be joy, peace, and many, many blessings. The narthex, like life, is a mixture of good and bad, pain and pleasure, joy and sorrow.

I often wonder what the narthex of life would be like without what happens in the chancel.

It's worth pondering.

A FULL BARN OR A FULL LIFE

After moving to our new home, my wife decided to refinish an old chair. It was not an easy task because this chair was covered in layers of paint of different colors. A combination of sandpaper, steel wool, liquid stripper, and elbow grease has yet to remove all of the heavily sealed paint. The strongest bonding glue that ever came from Elmer's factory could not have a tighter bond. For days, Janene worked on that old chair.

It is not a fancy chair—quite the opposite. It is a rather plain rocker with a cane bottom and no arms. The back is slightly curved for a comfortable fit. It sits rather low, thereby making it more appropriate for a person with short legs. It was not made for watching TV or reading. It will not recline in ten different positions. It is not overstuffed; it has no stuffing whatsoever.

If we tried to sell this rocker at a yard sale, it would bring ten dollars or less. However, Janene would not take twenty times that much. She has developed a strong attachment to that piece of furniture, not because of its market value, but because of the one for whom it was purchased. This chair is significant because it belonged to Janene's Grandmother Dunavant who used it to rock her young children to sleep.

Maybe the chair would not mean so much if Grandmother Dunavant had not been such a good woman. From the Dunavant oral tradition, I have learned that Grandmother Dunavant believed that the more you give away in love, the more you have. According to the standards of this world, Grandmother Dunavant never had much, but she was rich. She did not have a full barn, but she had a full life.

It's worth pondering.

★ CATFISH AND CHRISTIANITY

He stood alone in the tee box. He was tall, muscular, and bearded, with no golfing companions in sight.

"Bud," I said, "is he playing solo?" Bud nodded and then invited the stranger to play the next nine holes with us. As we played, I learned he was from Ohio and was going to graduate school in Nashville with the support of the GI Bill. So friendly and engaging was this chap that I decided to tease him.

After about five holes I said, "If you stay in Nashville long enough, we'll teach you to eat black-eyed peas, grits, cornbread, and catfish."

"I like German food," he responded pointedly. So abrupt was his retort that I carefully put the dietary habits of Southerners on the back burner. As he walked the fairway to the last green, he approached me and asked in a whisper, "Do you really eat catfish?" I nodded in the affirmative. "Really?" Again, I motioned in the positive, growing curious at his insistence. "How could you?" he exclaimed. "Back home we throw them back or feed them to the cats."

Our regional food preferences are but one small indication of the differences that exist among individuals. We are not different altogether by choice but because our backgrounds and cultures have molded us to see life differently. We hold various views, cling to divergent political philosophies, practice certain customs, and accept different images of God. We notice our differences in the global village, throughout our neighborhood, and around our family dinner table. We can no longer afford to run from these differences, fight them, or ignore them. They need to be acknowledged so that we can understand one another.

Christianity proclaims that God came in Christ to transcend our differences and thereby make us one. Christ came not to make us carbon copies of one another but to bring us compassionately together.

It's worth pondering.

✦ BEING STILL, KNOWING GOD

Being busy is not a virtue, but as a culture we are always talking about how busy we are. A sense of hurry pervades much of life. Once while standing outside a church classroom where a course was being taught on "The Hurried Family," I overheard a wife say to her husband, "Please hurry or we will never make it"—right after a class devoted to overcoming hurry in a hurried world!

This compulsion to hurry is so acute that we feel uncomfortable when we are not going at a fast pace. One of my parishioners said that the only time she allows herself to stop is while others are being served Holy Communion on the first Sunday of each month. For some, this might be opportunity for reflection, meditation, and prayer. It is not that people do not care about such things, it is that time often equals achievement, success, or money. If a minute or an hour is lost, we feel guilty. At best, that is pitiful, absolutely pitiful.

This sense of hurry does something to us—more than deplete our energy or make us weary. Hurriedness in life disqualifies us for the work of conversation and prayer that develops the relationships that meet the most profound human need. There are heavy demands put upon our work, true; there is difficult work to be engaged in, yes. But the thoughtful Christian, if he or she is to serve others, need not always be busy.

Maybe that is why the scripture says, "Be still, and know that I am God'" (Ps. 46:10).

It's worth pondering.

✴ SOLUTIONS

Our society needs a growing number of believers who will look for the meaning in the happenings of everyday life as they read the paper, watch TV, or listen to the news.

Take, for example, the horrible violence that we see displayed almost every day by the media all over the globe. What does it mean and what does it tell us about the human condition? Does the violence tell us that we have become depersonalized? Does it tell us that we see each other as "its" and not as "thous"? Does it tell us that the sacredness of human life is not valued in our culture? Or does it tell us that some people will use violence as a means to an end?

Certainly, violence tells us that many in our culture do not see others as God sees them. Rather, the perpetrators of violence must see other persons as a means to an end, as a way of getting what they want, and not as companions on life's journey.

To put it bluntly, violence is telling us that life is not right. It is telling us that we have not yet learned how to love. It is telling us that a great void and vacuum exists in many persons' lives. It is telling us that many persons in our society have not learned to live by the greater and nobler way of mercy, justice, and compassion.

What, then, is the answer to violence? I hold to the notion that the Christian faith has the answer to violence, and the answer to violence is sacrificial love—the kind of love that we see in the life and teachings of Jesus Christ. It is our task as the church to model a better and different way of life.

Almost everyone is looking for a solution to violence: politicians, educators, social scientists, psychologists, psychiatrists, and family leaders. But in my judgment, we do not have to look for a solution to violence. That solution has already been given. It goes something like this: "'In everything do to others as you would have them do to you'" (Matt. 7:12). It was spoken a long time ago by a man from Nazareth, Jesus Christ.

It's worth pondering.

 LEAVE YOUR PAST WITH GOD

I often find myself reflecting on the past. I spend a fair portion of almost every Monday morning reworking my Sunday sermon. I ask myself, *Was I true to the text? Could I have found a better illustration or quote? What could have gone unsaid? Was the Good News proclaimed?* After considering questions like these, I often feel that I could preach a better sermon on Monday than on the preceding Sunday.

During my daily devotional time, I came across a sentence in the book *The Christian's Secret of a Happy Life* by Hannah Whitall Smith that resonated with me. She writes, "Never indulge, at the close of an action, in any self-reflective acts of any kind, whether of self-congratulation or of self-despair. Forget the things that are behind, the moment they are past, leaving them with God."*

I, for one, need to hear and heed Smith's insight because I tend to indulge myself in evaluating and replaying moments in my life that have already gone by. Rather than reliving the words or deeds, I would do better if I honestly turned them over to the Lord to forgive my mistakes and to bless my efforts. If I could do this, there would be fewer "blue Mondays" or times of depression.

This is not to say that we should not evaluate our past actions and decisions. But it is to say that we should make every effort not to keep our past as current as the morning paper.

It's worth pondering.

---

*Smith, Hannah W., *The Christian's Secret of a Happy Life* (Brownstone Books, 2009), 74.

✹ SATURDAY AND SUNDAY

They sat two tables away from me. And they sat side by side. They ate their sausage biscuits as if they were inhaling, not chewing. Both were dressed in baseball uniforms, complete with matching caps and shirts. As I watched them and listened to them talk baseball, I puzzled about what was going on between that father and son.

Appearances would say that they had a lot in common—baseball, breakfast, and the sheer pleasure of sharing time together. The father seemed to know what his son was thinking and feeling, and the son seemed pleased that his dad joined him in his "little league" world.

I began thinking about what their relationship might become in the future. Would they always hold something in common, or would they drift apart? Would they grow in their relationship, or would their relationship diminish over time? Would they always enjoy Saturday morning breakfast, baseball, and each other's company? Would there be something or someone that brings mutual satisfaction to both?

Or would something or someone come between them? Would the son become shaped by a different story? A story not known or understood by his father. A story filled with different characters shaped around a vague and obscure plot. A story whose ideology ran contrary to the values and beliefs of the father.

Would the father's life become shaped by a different story? A story that involved another job or moving to another part of the country. A story that contained fewer convictions and a lessened understanding of what life really means.

Would the son grow up and live his life apart from the influence of his father? Would the relationship remain strong and vital in spite of the competing stories that would shape the life of each?

The next day, I saw the same father and son sitting side by side in the sanctuary. They sang together, read together, listened together, and took the bread and cup together.

The father has his priorities right. He knows the importance of being with his son on the ball field on Saturday and of sharing a time of worship with his son on Sunday.

I know other fathers who join their sons in holding the bat and glove but rarely, if ever, join their sons in holding the hymnal, the bread, and the cup.

It's worth pondering.

HAPPINESS THROUGH GIVING

Our culture teaches us that the happiest and most fulfilled individuals are those who acquire more and more. I find the reverse to be true. In all my years of ministry, I've found that the happiest persons are those who witness to their faith by more and more sharing. To me, this truth may seem simple enough. Yet, it seems to be a difficult lesson to learn.

Marriages break up because spouses do not give to each other. Children become separated from their parents because giving is absent in the relationship. The congregation that does not give to its community begins to die.

God wanted the children of Israel to be a light to the world. Instead, they kept the light for themselves, and they moved steadily toward the loss of identity as the people of God. Jesus asked his followers to be the light of the world. But some of them put the light under the bushel—which is just a way of saying that they kept it for themselves—and the light was extinguished. Life does not go well when we do not give to each other.

I have decided that God does not care whether or not we raise the budgets of our churches. But God does care passionately about how we give to others. When we do not give, we are living contrary to the way God created us. As Paul reminds us in 2 Corinthians 9:7, "God loves a cheerful giver."

I believe that God wants us to find happiness, and the tried-and-true way to find happiness is by giving to others.

As a pastor to thousands of people, I have discovered that those who give of their financial resources and of themselves are the happiest persons on earth.

It's worth pondering.

✦ WHAT DYING PEOPLE TALK ABOUT

I took my first appointment as a pastor in 1959, and since that time, I have had many opportunities to speak with congregants who are in the process of dying.

I've found that at the end of their lives, persons rarely want to discuss their achievements, successes, or their possessions. They don't talk about their golf swing, their clothing, or the make of their cars. They never discuss politics or "church business."

Some have wanted to talk about unfinished business—a deep regret or an unfulfilled wish. Others have wanted to confess sin and receive Holy Communion. A few have discussed a fear of death and its possible consequences.

Mainly, though, these deathbed conversations have been about family—sons, daughters, sisters, brothers, mothers, and fathers. We discuss the support and care offered by friends, church members, and Sunday school classes. Persons marvel about the blessings of love, both given and received.

I end each visit in the same way: I ask to say a prayer. In all my years as a pastor, very few have refused this offer. As I begin to pray, he or she will gently put a hand in mine—sometimes both hands—and we pray together for the last time.

It's worth pondering.

✦ LOVING YOUR ENEMIES

The teachings of our culture do not call us to love our enemies. As a culture, we commonly practice retaliation and revenge instead of forgiveness and reconciliation. We believe that "an eye for an eye" is the best method of justice.

The teachings of Jesus challenge us to live by a different ethic. He said, "You have heard that it was said, 'You shall love your neighbor and hate your enemy.' But I say to you, Love your enemies and pray for those who persecute you" (Matt. 5:43-44). This kind of love is impossible without God. From God, we learned how to love, for God loved us first. As we begin to share this love with others—perhaps even those some might call "unlovable"—we make it possible for other persons to become loving as well.

The more we surrender ourselves to God's grace, the more we are made able to love all people, including our enemies.

It's worth pondering.

BELIEF
and
FAITH

RAYMOND, RUDOLPH, AND OTIE

It's been many years since I participated in a groundbreaking for the building of a new sanctuary, but I will never forget the experience.

In my first assignment as a student-pastor, I served a rural congregation called Gratitude that had about seventy-five members. Most of the members were well beyond sixty-five years of age, and there were very few children or young persons. The old building had been standing for almost one hundred years and had not been kept in good repair. Paint peeled. Floors sagged. Pews were split. Carpet was torn. No running water or restrooms could be found inside the building.

Some church members thought that the congregation should close and merge with a nearby church. Others thought that we should patch up the dilapidated building. Another group thought that we should build a new church. It was, by every measure, a tough decision.

The "Official Board," as we called it, met again and again, trying to make a decision that would reflect the best interests of all concerned. The decision was made harder because the members of the board loved one another and did not want to hurt another person's feelings. In addition, everyone was kin to everyone else, so both blood and emotions were wound together.

I remember the night that the decision was made. After a long and often heated discussion, Rudolph Williams stood up and said, "If Otie Tims will give $500, I'll give $500." That was it. The ball was now in the court of Otie Tims, the oldest man in the church. Mr. Otie, as we called him, did not stand, but when he started to speak everyone gave ear.

"I'll match Rudolph and then some," he said. "Most of us are older, and we will not need a new building for very long. We do not have many children and youth in this congregation, but we must build a new church. Someday the city will be moving in this direction, and I want to have a nice building here for those who will someday come."

Others spoke and pledged their support. After a long discussion, Raymond Williams, Rudolph's brother, said, "We've jawed about this for years—let's vote." The vote was close, but the decision to build carried. Some said it could never be done. Others said it could. Some said that the money could be better spent. Some were satisfied with the old building and the old ways.

Those who wanted to make room for others went to work hosting bake sales, barbeque dinners, quilting bees, ice cream suppers, and car washes. Likewise, church members dug into their savings accounts and set aside a portion of their income for that which was yet to be.

Not one of those people who sat in the Board meeting on that hot summer's night in 1959 is still at Gratitude Church. They have all been transported to the Church Eternal.

Last fall I ran into a woman who was only thirteen years of age when the decision was made. I learned that she and her son are now every-Sunday members of Gratitude Church. I inquired about the congregation. Since 1959, the church has grown in membership, and a fellowship hall and Sunday school classrooms were added. In our conversation, she mentioned various people who now belong to the church. Except for her son, I did not recognize one name.

The night that Rudolph stood up and pledged $500 was a historic moment in the life of that tiny church. Later I learned that Rudolph Williams did not have $100—much less $500—on the night of that church meeting. The next day he went to the bank and floated a loan, not knowing how he would pay it back.

A mixture of fear and hope filled the air on the day that we broke ground at Gratitude Church. Some cried and some shouted, but all of us knew that we were making room for those whose names we would never know. All of us knew that we had to position ourselves to offer Christ to what would someday become a growing community.

At groundbreaking, Otie Tims turned the first spade of dirt. As Otie pushed the shovel into the rich West Tennessee soil, Rudolph smiled as big as he could. In their hearts, both men knew that they were giving birth to a future that would someday belong to whoever might pass that way.

It's worth pondering.

⭐ IN WHOM WILL WE BELIEVE?

It is human nature to want to believe in something. Our desire to believe in something is as natural as breathing. Faith is instinctive. In my experience, people not only want to believe, they do believe in something or someone.

If people do not believe in God, they will believe in success, power, or prestige. And some who do not believe in God choose to have faith in themselves.

I once heard a speaker posit that the real religion in America is winning or being "number one." In my opinion, there is nothing inherently wrong with being first or the best at some activity, but there is something wrong with believing that first is the only place to be. It is sad not to do one's best, but it is not a mortal failure to do all that one can and still end up in second place.

I know that I have an odd view of things, but I would like to hear fans of a second place basketball team hold their fingers in the air and shout, "We're number two!" Sadly our culture values most those who finish in first place. Shouting "We're number two" might be viewed with great suspicion.

According to the Bible, it is not where you are in the pecking order that matters; what matters is whether or not love is present. Saint Paul said, "If I have all faith, so as to remove mountains, but do not have love, I am nothing" (1 Cor. 13:3). In our natural desire to put our faith in something, we often place it in something temporal like winning instead of something eternal like love.

The crucial question is not "Will we believe?" but "In whom will we believe?"

It's worth pondering.

★ PARKER'S QUESTIONS

A very nice six-year-old boy named Parker lives next door to me. Now and then he comes over to talk. We are slowly getting to know each other, and I don't know a lot about him yet. But one quality that is most apparent to me is that he is full of questions.

"Why are you watering that tree?" "When are you going to play golf again?" "How tall is your house?" "When are you going to wash your car?" These are some questions that Parker has posed.

I, for one, hope that Parker never ceases to ask questions because curiosity leads to finding answers. As he grows older, I would be pleased if he learns to ask crucial and important questions.

What we learn about life tends to fit the shape of our questions. If we ask shallow, superficial questions, we will have a view of life that lacks depth. People who come close to understanding the meaning of life are those who raise and pursue the more difficult questions.

Likewise, if our questions about God are narrowly based, our knowledge of God will be narrow. Too many believers treat God as a mascot, a hobby, or an acquaintance. They see God as their buddy, as "the man upstairs," or as a copilot. Such an understanding of God does not arise from reflective, thoughtful questioning.

An example of posing difficult questions comes in asking why an all-powerful and loving God would allow suffering, injustice, and evil in the world. Some would say that such questioning illustrates a lack of faith. But I suggest that asking difficult questions might be the prelude to creating and sustaining a strong and vital faith. I know many people who want a simple faith based on shallow, dogmatic statements. Yet, I also know many persons who hunger for a faith that allows them to ask the tough questions in life. I encourage you to seek a faith that can withstand the tough questions.

It's worth pondering.

✦ THE CROSS

After we committed my wife's aunt to her final resting place, Janene wanted to find the grave of her grandmother who was buried in the same hallowed ground. No one had been there for years, so it was difficult to remember the correct location. Some of the relatives thought it was to the east; some thought it to the west. No one was certain. As we walked along the grass-covered knoll, we passed marker after marker with names and dates stamped into cold, gray stone.

As we searched, I wondered why Janene wanted to view the stone. Was it to get in touch with childhood memories? To recall the goodness of a saintly woman? Or did she want to visit her grandmother's grave because she was known to be a believer?

People say, "I believe" (*credo* in Latin) to refer to God on Sunday, and again on Monday to express their opinions about the weather or the next election. But loving, humble belief cannot be taken so casually.

The word *believe* is rooted in the Old English *leof*, meaning "dear, cherished, loved, or longed for." Add the prefix *be-* (meaning "to cause to be"), and what we cherish causes our being—makes us who we are. Therefore, in believing we become what we long for.

I have yet to ask her, but maybe that is the reason that Janene wanted to stand in front of the stone—to reach back and get in touch with the spirit of a person who knew what should be held dear, cherished, loved, and longed for.

As Christians, we stand before another symbol—not a grave in a cemetery—but a cross. Like Janene going to her grandmother's grave, we must revisit the cross lest we forget the one from Nazareth who "cherished, loved, and longed for" God so much that he willingly sacrificed himself that we might experience the God who is far beyond us, but deep within us.

After a bit of searching we found the location of the earth-encased coffin. As we stood there, holding hands, we felt the presence of a sacrificial love that is not limited to time or place. Such is the cross.

It's worth pondering.

★ WHEN LIFE HAPPENS TO US

Despite all of our efforts, much of life happens to us. The big turning points in our lives do not occur because we sit in a long-range planning committee. Many pivotal events in our lives come as the result of interacting factors. We cannot forecast these factors, nor can we anticipate them. And more often than not, they are beyond our control.

Our Lord was no exception. To be sure, he made things happen in life. But life also happened to him. The political and religious leaders turned against him. The disciples deserted and denied him. The billowing tide of history seemed to turn against his teachings and that for which he stood.

In the face of life turning against him, Jesus kept the faith. He remained obedient to God; he did not waver.

When life turns against the grain, we, like our Lord, need to remain steadfast, true, obedient, and loyal to God. Drawing upon and relying on our religious resources will get us through even the darkest hours of life.

At such times it is important for us to slow down, remember our values, trust friends, and believe with all of our heart that even the darkest hour is not the last hour.

The God who brought life from the Cross is the same God who can bring hope and love to the crosses that we bear.

It's worth pondering.

THE GREATNESS OF JESUS

There are moments when I think solely about Christ—nothing more and nothing less. Just Christ. I think about how he is too big for us. Jesus did not fit into the narrow definition of culture and propriety. The petty loyalties, the tight limits, and the tunnel vision of those surrounding him could not confine him. He would not stay inside their narrow limits, legalisms, rituals, silly conventions, and provincial attitudes. He was too large for them, and he is too big for our boxed-in understanding of how things are, or how we think they ought to be.

Jesus is marked by a special kind of greatness. He revealed a universal truth about the nature and purpose of God. The truth had been there all along, but Jesus revealed it and made it clear.

This Christ who is big and great is also inescapable. He is in every person, though some have not yet discovered him. John Wesley, the founder of Methodism, spoke of prevenient grace—God's grace found in every human being. It is the grace that precedes our coming to faith. Christ's influence in the world is beyond escape.

It's worth pondering.

 SHEILAISM

Have you heard about a woman who named her religion after herself? If everyone in America did this, we would have over 311 million American religions, one for each of us.

Her name is Sheila Larson. She is a young nurse who says that she is not a religious fanatic. She proudly calls her religion "Sheilaism." She says, "I can't remember the last time I went to church. My faith has carried me a long way. It's Sheilaism. Just my own little voice."

In defining Sheilaism she said, "It's just trying to love yourself and be gentle with yourself. You know, I guess, take care of each other." There is nothing more or nothing less to Sheilaism!

Sadly, Sheilaism seems to be a perfectly natural expression of current American religious life and informs us of the role of religion in the United States today. Sheilaism is a watered-down view of religion. It calls for no serious commitment to Christ, God's church, or God's people. It is a religion that requires nothing—no cross, no sacrifice, no bearing one another's burdens, no reflection on what God requires of us; no giving of time, resources, or income to other persons.

Sheilaism can get along pretty well in the world. But this form of religion will have difficulty when trouble comes, when anxiety seems overwhelming, when others fail us, when the storms of doubt assail, or when the meaning of life is not understood.

Religion, at its best, is more than having one's own private faith. Religion grapples with what is best for the community. It reflects upon a larger responsibility for others. It labors for the common good.

For Christians, our faith is both private and public. We believe in a vital piety linked to a social responsibility for others.

John Wesley said that there is no such thing as a solely private religion. For him, all inward religion included a public expression of faith.

The writer of First John said, "Let us love one another, because love is from God; everyone who loves is born of God and knows God" (4:7).

Our expression of faith through love of God and others produces a vital life not attained through Sheilaism.

It's worth pondering.

THE ILLUSION OF KNOWLEDGE

Columbus did not know where he was going. When he sailed from Palos de la Frontera on the evening of August 3, 1492, he believed ocean covered only one-seventh of the globe. That was the conclusion of orthodox Christian authorities. He believed the western ocean narrowed, and that Asia extended farther eastward than it does. After all, many of his carefully studied geographies said so.

After four trips to the New World, he died believing he had been exploring the east coast of Asia. But his path of discovery eventually led Europeans to the knowledge that their certainties about geography were false.

The notable significance of the voyages is the discovery of the ancient people's ignorance of the world. The more people learned about the world, the more they knew how much they did not know.

In the early 70s, my wife and I made our first trip abroad. We went to Israel, Greece, and Italy. When we got home, people would ask us what we had learned about the Holy Land and other destinations. Though I never did, I wanted to tell my questioners that I learned how very little I knew.

What was true for Columbus and for me on my first trip abroad is also true of our understanding of God. The more we think we know about God only leads us to learn how little we actually know. I have been a serious student of scripture and Christian theology for most of my adult life. I have attempted to understand the meaning of life. I have pondered, wrestled, and reflected. My questing has led me to realize how little I know.

In recent days I have come to believe that one does not have to be a theology scholar in order to be a firm believer. If we want to see what God is like, we need look no further than Jesus of Nazareth. To know that God is love is enough for me. To believe that God, through the Holy Spirit, is present with us is enough for me. To know that I am known by God is enough for me.

It's worth pondering.

⭐ TOLERANCE

I know that people are no longer whipped through the streets of Boston for being Baptists. Nor are Quakers burned at the stake. Modern-day Methodists are not stoned while preaching as was John Wesley. However, there is a rise in religious intolerance.

Religious intolerance expresses itself as fundamentalism in most every major religion. Fundamentalism is dangerous because it is intolerant of other points of view. It has simplistic, black-and-white answers for complex problems. Fundamentalism is myopic and exclusive.

Intolerant people and groups do not believe that the truth can be trusted to win its own way if given a fair field. Such people believe that truth must be bolstered by artificial enforcements, heresy trials, personal discourtesy, defamation, and the practice of exclusion.

Tolerance, on the other hand, does not mean the absence of belief. Nor does it mean that we are not to believe strongly. Nor does it mean that all beliefs hold equal value. Tolerant persons are not those to whom all sides look alike. Rather, tolerant persons hold certain essential beliefs to be crucial, while being free to search for new truths and new insights. For example, a man who feels certain of his relationship with his wife is free from jealousy. So, a person who is certain of the truth can be courteous to rival opinions.

Great believers are those who hold to bedrock beliefs while extending grace and understanding to those of differing opinions. As Paul writes in his letter to the church at Ephesus, "With all humility and gentleness, with patience, [bear] with one another in love, making every effort to maintain the unity of the Spirit in the bond of peace" (Eph. 4:2-3).

It's worth pondering.

✹ UNANNOUNCED

One of my primary interests in ministry has been to help skeptics come to a living faith. As I prepare sermons or lessons, I am aware that there might be some person present who is sitting on the edge of belief. To enable that person to move from unbelief to belief is sometimes a short, but at other times a long, journey. Most of the time persons move toward Christianity through what one might call revelations—those fleeting moments when God's presence is real and certain.

These experiences may be triggered by a bar of music, a landscape, a note from a dear friend, or the surfacing of a forgotten memory.

A revelation gives us an instantaneous sense of seeing into the heart of life, as though a reality beyond all realities opened itself wide for an instant and, just as instantly, closed its door.

Most of us go for long periods of time unvisited by such revelatory experiences. Then, in rather surprising ways, they come unannounced and in full strength. These fleeting revelations of God's presence continue off and on for most of our lives.

When I was about twelve years old, I had such an experience while walking home from our neighborhood church. Except for the blinking of a few stars, the night sky was deep and dark. As I traveled toward home, a feeling of God's presence washed over me. I was not looking for it. It came unannounced.

This experience was not overpowering. It did not shake me to the foundations. Nor did it manifest itself as a bright, blinding light. As I look back on this pivotal moment, I realize I felt a gentle nudging of the Spirit. As I shared that holy moment with my pastor, he calmly assured me by saying, "Stay open, stay open." That is all that he said, but that was enough.

It's worth pondering.

LOVE
and
FRIENDSHIP

"KITCHEN TABLE" FRIENDS

One Sunday evening friends called to ask if they might come over for a few minutes. They didn't need to discuss anything in particular. They just wanted to check on how Janene and I were getting along. "Of course," I said, "we would be happy to see you."

After a short while the doorbell rang and in they came. Conversation started even before we could get seated before a roaring fire. Talk moved from topic to topic—our children, our respective congregations, a recently held birthday party, our health concerns.

Before we knew it, the time had come for supper. Janene offered a turkey sandwich. Our guests refused. She offered again. They said that they had not come to eat. This time I offered. Again they said, "No, we must go."

Janene said, "It's just a turkey sandwich, and it will not take but a minute to prepare, so please stay." They finally agreed, and off we went to the kitchen for turkey sandwiches and more conversation.

This story illustrates our relationship with our very best friends—we can serve them leftovers around the kitchen table. We don't need to be fancy; we can just be ourselves.

Life does not offer us many "kitchen table" friends, and we are thankful for those we do have. Who are the persons in your life with whom the serving of leftovers can become a sacrament?

It's worth pondering.

★ WHAT SUSTAINS US

What sustains us in life is very important. We are not sustained by position or power, though many persons build their lives around both. Nor are we sustained by entertainment, though many of us are entertaining ourselves to death. Nor are we sustained merely by hard work, though many are slaves to careers. Nor are we sustained by money, though for a fair number of people money has become a god. Even the good parts of life—family, music, art, literature—cannot serve to sustain us fully. All of these matters have their place, but none of them is sufficient for life.

We can only live from love because love is the only thing that cannot be destroyed. But it is not just any kind of love that makes life possible. It is sacrificial love that gives us life.

In the life and teachings of Jesus we see an example of sacrificial love. When we sacrificially live for one another, we have something for which to live. Practicing sacrificial love is not something that we can manufacture or produce. It comes from a loving God, whose very nature is love.

It's worth pondering.

★ SIMPLE, YET DIFFICULT

The Old Testament listed Ten Commandments. Jesus knew them by heart. No doubt he rehearsed them in his mind more times than he could remember. He must have pondered their meaning and applied them to his life. These commandments were riveted to his conscience.

Those who came to Jesus one day understood that he knew all ten of the commandments. But they wanted to know which of the ten he thought to be the most important. Hearing their question, Jesus said, "'You shall love the Lord your God with all your heart, and with all your soul, and with all your mind.' This is the greatest and first commandment. And a second is like it: 'You shall love your neighbor as yourself.' On these two commandments hang all the law and the prophets" (Matt. 22:37-40).

Jesus' answer has gone down in the annals of theology as the Great Commandment. It is simple. It is twofold. It is easily memorized.

This commandment, "the Great One," is easy to learn and easy to understand, but it can be difficult to keep.

It is not easy to keep the Great Commandment because we do not have within ourselves the power to do so. We do not have the strength, the will, or the moral mettle to live up to this high standard. By our own muscle and wit, we cannot live out the meaning of loving God and loving our neighbor.

But if we are going to love God and our neighbor, we must start somewhere. We need to begin by admitting how challenging it is to love this way. Own it. Say it to ourselves. Say it to God.

The next step is letting God work through us. It is God working through us that enables us to love this way. If God does not move through us, it will be impossible to love God and our neighbor.

In a word, we need to be transformed by the Holy One if we are to keep this Great Commandment. The one who gives us the Great Commandment is the very one who enables us to keep it.

It's worth pondering.

★ THE ARRIVAL OF LOVE

I know a sixty-year-old man whose wife recently asked him for a divorce. She fell in love with the next-door neighbor who happened to be a prominent person in the community. The divorce was very painful for both parties but especially for the husband.

For months the man grieved over the loss of his wife, to whom he had been married for about forty years. He complained of not feeling well. His place of business, an old gas station, became rundown and in need of repair. His yard, once a showplace, started looking more like a weed patch. He complained of poor eyesight but refused to go to the physician for much-needed attention. An untended pulled muscle in his leg led to the development of a noticeable limp.

About two years after the divorce he met a lovely and thoughtful woman. Sparks flew. Feeling was there. They enjoyed the pleasure of each other's company.

Then a miracle happened. He decided to go to the eye doctor. He began exercising regularly, which eased the limp. His yard was cleaned and prettier than ever. The old service station got a new roof and a paint job. The grief passed, and he started living again.

Therein lies one of the mysteries of human love. Love can expand and rebuild a broken human spirit. The freely given love of another person gives birth to something in us that cannot be contained. The barriers that we have erected to protect ourselves against disappointment and humiliation come tumbling down. The unmistakable sign of love in us is our willingness to be renewed in our relationship to others.

A fundamental teaching of the Christian faith is that God loves us. In fact, God not only loves us, God delights in us and yearns for us to accept divine love for ourselves and to love others as God loves us.

The writer of First John put it like this, "Let us love one another, because love is from God. . . . Since God loved us so much, we also ought to love one another" (4:7, 11).

It's worth pondering.

⭐ WHAT'S WRONG WITH THAT?

His name was Montie—at least, that's what everyone called him. He always wore work clothes with a railroad cap perched on top of his head.

Montie was our volunteer "Mr. Fix-It" at the church I was serving. He'd come over to the church almost every day to see what we needed to have painted or repaired. If a light switch wouldn't work, we would say, "Let Montie fix it." No matter what—carpentry, plumbing, roofing, masonry, or painting—Montie would always tackle the task.

As far as I know, Montie never took a dime for his labor. If it was going to be a big job that required an extra pair of hands, he would bring Pearle with him. Pearle was his wife of some fifty-plus years. Montie said that she was as good a helper as one would ever want.

I had one problem with Montie. It was not the quality of his work or the length of time it took to complete a project or his attitude. My vexation with him was that no matter what he had accomplished, he would always want one of the clergy to look at what he had done. No matter what I was doing, Montie would interrupt me to show off what he had repaired. I could recognize his shuffling steps coming down the hall, and I knew that I was going to be pulled away from my labor to see the results of his.

After showing me the work, Montie's question was always the same: "What's wrong with that?" He would say this proudly as he pointed at the job. The greater problem was that Montie would not wait until he had finished a task before he would pull me away from my desk to show me what he had done. He would paint one strip, fix one board, patch one hole, tighten one nut, repair one switch, and then he would take me or whomever he could find, and ask, "What's wrong with that?" With Montie's good work, there was nothing "wrong with that," so I would pat him on the back for a job well done.

Growth in God's church occurs because there are many Monties—people who love the church and who do what they can to help it continue the work of Christ on earth. "What's wrong with that?"

It's worth pondering.

⭐ REEBOKS AND A REAL FRIEND

One morning I went for a jog while visiting a large city. I was well equipped with running shoes and a sweater for warmth. I had everything I needed—except my glasses. At one point, I stopped my run to go inside an open church.

As I sat in a pew for a time of prayer and reflection, I automatically reached for a booklet that was lying on the hardwood pew. Without my glasses, though, I could not read it. Letters and words blurred together into one glob of a paragraph. I squinted, turned my head this way and that, and moved the page forward and back, but I could not make out even one complete sentence.

Since I was unable to read, I found myself deep in thought. Time passed quickly. Memories of loved ones and events flooded my being, and I experienced a sure sense of God's presence. The mystics would call it a transcendental experience. Some would say that I experienced the Holy One. I call it a genuine God connection.

To me, God's presence is that of a caring friend. Some people see God as a wrathful judge. Some as a distant creator. Some as love. Some as a strong father. Some as a nurturing mother. At times I have experienced God in all of these ways and more. But on that morning, I felt God's friendship.

A true friend is one with whom we can unburden ourselves and know that we are going to be heard and accepted regardless of what we say or feel. A friend is one who instinctively accepts the otherwise unacceptable in us.

A friendship is an unpretentious relationship, for friend is not a designation of office nor a function one must perform from time to time nor a role one is supposed to play in society. Friendship is personal; it combines both affection and respect.

In addition, friends are persons who listen. And so, if we think of God as a friend, we will see God as one who cares enough to listen, to care, and to answer.

It's worth pondering.

THE
CHURCH

✦ THE CHURCH'S MISSION

If "hell" means separation from God, the world in which we live is stuck in what the ancient Hebrews called "sheol." Our social, domestic, and personal problems are scaling the heights. Within the church I hear two approaches to handling these issues.

One approach lies with those who feel that such problems reside wholly outside the church's mission. They understand the religious enterprise as pertaining exclusively to God, the soul, and eternity. Church is a place to get away from the agonies of life, not a place to struggle with them.

Some people say that they attend church to forget the problems of the outside world. Said one such person, "What I want in this sanctuary is a moratorium on complexity. I want to hear about the majesty of God and what I have to look forward to in the next life. I wish you would preach more on the book of Revelation and when the end is going to come. That is what excites me—when this whole sorry mess of history is going to be over, and we get to the place of peace and joy."

The other approach lies with those who believe that facing issues that persons encounter every day—crime, racism, mental illness, moral failure, sexism, and addiction—is within the framework of the church's purpose and calling.

These persons become restless with "God talk" that does not scratch where they itch. Rituals of worship and prayer that do not connect with real life are of little value to them. Such persons say that if the church cannot provide tools for facing the struggles of the real world, they will turn away from an irrelevant institution. Finding ways to show that the teachings of Jesus are applicable to the real lives of real people is imperative.

In my opinion, both of these approaches are valid. Christianity must feed the soul without neglecting the daily, down-to-earth issues and needs of the human condition. To have one without the other is just not practical.

It's worth pondering.

 CHANGE THE QUESTION

As time passes, questions change. Thirty years ago when I became a pastor, the primary faith question was "Is it true?" College students, teachers, scientists, and others wanted to know the truth as presented by Christianity. Study groups, classes, conferences, and conversations went on and on about the convictions and claims of Christianity.

The atmosphere was so alive with questions that I completed a thesis aiming to determine what people believe and how the church, through preaching and education, could help clarify and strengthen those beliefs.

Today, the questions are different. In the church, as in much of life, "Who benefits?" is more important than the validity of certain beliefs. So the primary question becomes, "How can the church benefit me?" For this reason, we see persons "shopping" for congregations that can provide the most.

If local congregations buy into this mentality, the temptation will be to market the church like a secular product. Churches will focus on marketing strategies that hope to bring in key demographics of church-goers instead of focusing on the basic spiritual needs of their congregants and communities.

Our purpose is not to market the institutional church like one would market a new restaurant. We have a larger purpose: to help connect persons to God and one another through Jesus Christ. To be sure, we need to do that in understandable and meaningful ways, but we cannot "sell" the gospel. We can only bear witness to its power to change lives.

Asking ourselves what we believe about God and what God wants to do through us is more important than "How can I benefit?"

It's worth pondering.

✦ KNOWING AND FOLLOWING

Observing life and listening closely can be quite revealing. While strolling through the foyer of a church, I overheard a woman saying to a child, "The church is where we are taught the religion about Jesus."

The woman's observation set my mind to spinning. Now that I have reflected on her statement, I am not certain that she was on target.

The church is where we teach the religion *of* Jesus as distinguished from the religion *about* Jesus. To be certain, much in Christianity is *about* Jesus—things said of and believed concerning Jesus, theories to account for him, and accumulated explanations and interpretations of his life.

The larger task is to introduce people to the religion *of* Jesus—the religion by which Jesus lived. His filial fellowship with God. His purity, unselfishness, sincerity, sacrifice; his exaltation of spiritual values; and his unqualified love of others.

There is a vast difference in knowing about Jesus and in truly following the teachings of Jesus' life.

It's worth pondering.

 YOU CAN'T DESTROY A CHURCH

A building may be burned down, but a church cannot be extinguished. A Christian church is composed of people who believe that Christ is Lord. It is a community of persons who worship the God of Jesus of Nazareth. Its message is the good news that the grace displayed in the life and teachings of Jesus is available to all persons and that grace is the basis for the redemption of humankind. Its ethic is rooted in what love requires of all persons. Its hope is in the final triumph of righteousness. Its fellowship is open to people of all ages, races, and nations. It stands firmly against evil, injustice, and oppression in whatever forms they present themselves. It believes that there is no place where God is not. This—and much more—is what the church is, and it cannot be destroyed by fire, threat, terror, or crucifixion.

The building where a church gathers for worship, study, and prayer can be burned in the dark of night, but the church cannot and will not be eliminated from the landscape of any community. Those who burn church buildings—whether Christian churches, Jewish or Hindu temples, Muslim mosques, and so forth—do so with the false notion that intimidation, fear, and destruction have the power to both silence and break the spirit of a community. However, the reverse is true. With every fire, there is a new determination to be the community of faith. With every blaze leaping into the night sky, there is a brighter and stronger fire burning in the hearts of those who understand the true nature and purpose of the church. For every arsonist, there are untold numbers who believe that love is stronger than the threat of death.

Every time I read about another building going up in flames, I resolve again to stand against the evil that moves people toward destroying the places where we profess our faith. We must do all that we can to help with the rebuilding of these sacred spaces.

It's worth pondering.

CHRISTIAN
LIVING

⭐ LAUGHTER: A GIFT FROM GOD

Many people see the church as a rather dull place—a place where folks are somber, lifeless, and anything but joyous. But I find much amusement in the day-to-day events of the church. A few of these events are worth mentioning.

At my church's Vacation Bible School, a teacher explained the types of foods that were eaten in Jesus' day. She said that boys and girls ate figs, cheese, unleavened bread, fish, fruit, and they drank goat's milk. After hearing the menu, one child popped up and said, "Yuck, poor Jesus." What Jesus ate was a long way from the hamburgers and French fries to which the child was accustomed.

One Sunday morning the organist was playing a loud fanfarish piece for the prelude. It was just after Easter, and the organist was trying to establish the joyful mood reflected in the Resurrection. Although it was a glorious presentation, one lad had his hands cupped over his ears. From where I was sitting, I had a good angle on the little boy. When the organist had finished, the youngster looked up at his mother and said, "Thank you, God." He was not giving thanks for the prelude but for the fact that it was finally over!

While I served as the associate pastor of a church during the mid-'60s, the senior pastor made a terrible—and still talked about—blunder. The sanctuary had recently been adorned with a new tapestry that hung from floor to ceiling directly behind the pulpit and choir loft. When it was presented to the church, the senior pastor publicly thanked the generous donor for the lovely gift. In his concluding remarks he said, "As we come here to worship, I want all of us to be inspired by the lovely tapestry which hangs in my rear." The congregation broke out in laughter, and the pastor, though embarrassed, was big enough to laugh with them.

Laughter must be of God because it is good for the soul. It softens the heart and creates a greater spirit of reconciliation and openness.

If laughter is good for us and if it is of God, may we recognize times we experience humor and joy and thank God for them.

It's worth pondering.

 THAT WHICH CANNOT BE FRAMED

He has a wonderful and tastefully appointed library. Books artfully line the shelves like each one had been specifically ordered for a particular spot. Nothing is out of place; everything is in order. That's the way it is in his study.

Plaques and photographs hang on the paneled walls, reminders of accomplishments and important people he has met. He is photographed with Presidents Ronald Reagan and Gerald Ford. There are three handsome plaques given by the Tennessee School Boards Association "For Excellent Legislative Efforts in Support of Public Education." Memphis State University gave him the "Milestone of Excellence Award," and Millington First United Methodist Church awarded him two plaques—one for being the choir director for fifty years and one for teaching Sunday school for fifty-one years. Most of plaques and photos are arranged near a photograph of the Tennessee State Capitol where he served in the General Assembly for twenty-seven years.

As notable as the photographs and plaques are, they do not tell about his most important accomplishments. The transcendent part of him—his ethos, his values, his wit—cannot be framed or hung.

What is true for him is true for all persons: that which cannot be reduced to a wall hanging is more important than that which can.

A couple of weeks ago when he was coming out of a coma, I said, "Pops, I was in your study this morning, and I looked at all of the wall hangings, and I want to know which one is the most important to you."

Without blinking, Janene's father replied, "Never allow yourself to be impressed by your successes."

It's worth pondering.

⭐ GOD TURNS TOWARD US

The Old Testament prophets believed that if people did not repent of sin, life would get worse and not better. Refusal to repent would bring doom and darkness. Failure to repent would result in less love in the hearts of people.

On the other hand, these Hebrew prophets believed that if persons did repent, life would get better and not worse. Repentance would bring about a "day of the LORD," where persons would be restored to God and to one another.

For the Old Testament writers and for Jesus, repentance was possible because of God's steadfast love. Repentance was not a tit-for-tat transaction. It was and is possible only because God has already turned toward us, even before we consider turning toward the Holy One.

God turned toward us at the Cross and at the Resurrection. God is present with us in the breaking of bread and the serving of wine. God is revealed to us through the reading and proclaiming of scripture. God is shared with us in deeds of love and kindness. Thankfully, we can return to the Lord through repentance because God graciously leans in our direction. We do not have to get God's attention; we already have it.

It's worth pondering.

⭐ GOOD PEOPLE

As a pastor, I come into contact with many good people. I experience compassion from those who go the extra mile, take the high road, and extend generosity without any thought of receiving anything in return.

I hear people say kind words like *Thank you, Please, May I help?, You are doing a great job!,* and *Be good to yourself.*

I watch people listening to others— listening to hurts, hopes, fears, anxieties, and wishes. I see people coming to the aid of others when there is death, sickness, defeat, or loss. People do reach out. People do care. People do show concern. To put it bluntly, there is a mountain of good, well-intentioned people in the world.

If there is another side to the coin, it is that we tend to be good until our own self-interest is at stake. When self-interest is threatened, our hands can become clubs; our feet can became weapons; our tongues can become knives; and our consciences can become compromised.

There are times in life when our self-interest must be put aside in order to uplift others. It is not easy, but life calls us to make sacrifices for others, which is the highest form of love.

It is a sad and terrible commentary on our generation that in spite of all of the good people, more and more of us allow self-interest to override what is best for our family, our community, our nation, and the church.

It's worth pondering.

HAPPINESS AND FAITH

Maybe it is my age or my stage of life, but I have found myself thinking about what makes for happiness. The culture tells us that we cannot be happy unless we drive a particular car, vacation in a certain place, send our children to a brand-name school, live in a popular neighborhood, or obtain a highly sought-after career.

We are told by advertisers, TV commercials, social media, and a thousand hidden persuaders that we can find happiness if we search for it. So people search for happiness down the roads of pleasure, sex, marriage, work, drugs, travel, social service, and even religion.

People who believe that happiness can be sought and found are forever seeking change. Changing jobs, spouses, houses, communities, churches, as if a change in scenery will provide happiness.

There is a reason that happiness cannot be found by chasing it. The reason is that we carry our happiness or unhappiness inside us. Therefore, we take it into every new situation.

Happiness flows from the inside out and not from the outside in. Likewise, happiness does not come from something that we own or purchase. I have never bought one thing that made me happy. I have bought things that were useful or gave me pleasure but "having" does not bring happiness.

Too many people believe that happiness is the goal of life. But the goal of life is not to be happy. If we understand happiness to be the goal of life, we will be forever frustrated and anxious. Rather, the goal of life is to be good, loving, humble, and just. These are the qualities upon which God would have us focus. Happiness, in my opinion, is the by-product of goodness, compassion, humility, and fairness. That is where most of our thoughts and energy should go if we are to know the joy that comes from within.

So, do not search for happiness. Let it be the by-product of that which is deeply and yet profoundly within us.

It's worth pondering.

✦ TRUST IN THE LORD

My Sunday morning custom is to leave home early, stop for a big break-fast, and head for the church. One Sunday morning, I sat at the counter of an all-night diner and listened to a man who had made a killing in real estate ventures. This man clearly mistook luck for success. He was full of a confidence that made me believe that, to his mind, he had never been wrong. He knew why the stock exchange was sluggish. He knew why the University of Tennessee's football team was not winning. He spoke authoritatively on politics, international affairs, and religion. He understood why farmers were not making more money and why the U.S. economy was facing a recession.

Isn't it strange how listening to our own opinions can give us the assurance of wisdom for which philosophers search in vain? Because this man had been fortunate in one area, he knew something about everything and everything about most things. But, as we are reminded in Proverbs, it is better to "Trust in the LORD with all your heart, and do not rely on your own insight" (3:5).

It's worth pondering.

✦ THE INNER LIFE

There once lived a "knight of faith" in Denmark. It was often rumored that there was no greater Christian in all of Denmark than this noble knight. Spies were sent out to discover how he lived and what he said. Yet, all they found was a "complacent burgher" who could not be distinguished from his neighbors by the way he looked, talked, or conducted his life. The spies returned saying that the knight seemed no different from others through outward appearances.

The spies went to a wise Christian to determine how they were to know what it was that made the knight such a great Christian. The wise old believer instructed his questioners not to look to the outward forms, whether saintly or common, but to the inward "movements of infinity" that have no outward expression.

What distinguished that knight from all others is a trait so deep and personal that it cannot be outwardly observed or directly communicated. The Christian life is discerned and fostered by its substance and not its form.

It is this difficult-to-define substance that has much to do with the Christian life. Wesleyan heritage teaches us that it is the spirit or inner principle of Christ's life that becomes in us the Christian life.

Our life is a Christian life when we identify, recognize, focus on, and draw close to this life—the Holy One—who comes to us.

It is this inward riveting of our two lives that allows him to be Christ and us to be Christians; him to live his Christ-life and us to live our Christian lives.

So the outer forms of our Christian lives may differ radically. But our inner lives must focus on God.

It's worth pondering.

★ TRASH TALK

Trash-talk TV is a problem. Much of it is an exhibition of outrageous, bizarre, and often deviant behavior that is aired under the guise of entertainment and enlightenment. If the producers of these shows were to depict the positive and compassionate sides of the human condition, they would run the risk of losing a portion of their audiences.

Trash talk can even be witnessed at a more everyday level in the lack of respect and courtesy that is evidenced in everyday speech. On Halloween, for instance, a great number of children came by asking for treats, but very few said, "Thank you." Only two of the children said, "Sir." "Yeah" and "Nawh" were the expressions of choice. More than one child addressed me as "Dude." When I put the candy in one child's sack, the youngster responded by saying, "Cheap." There was not much evidence of deference, courtesy, or respect for the generosity and feelings of others.

In adults as in children, graciousness in speech is often absent. Talking down to one another is accepted. Talking *about* instead of *with* each other is commonplace. The courtesy of warm, loving speech is a foreign language to many people.

I am concerned about how we talk because words shape reality, and our speech can hurt or heal. As we follow Christ, we should work overtime to use language that helps and heals, rather than words that show no consideration for the feelings of others.

In writing to the Church at Colossae Paul said, "Let your speech always be gracious, seasoned with salt, so that you may know how you ought to answer everyone" (Col. 4:6).

It's worth pondering.

SPIRITUAL
GROWTH

✴ A SPIRITUAL JOURNEY

A few years ago, I took a spiritual journey. Something profound was stirring inside of me, and I realized that I wanted to know more about myself. I had a desire to go inside myself to see if I could discover the person within the person. I needed to find my own voice.

My journey took me down the roads of my childhood and my youth and my adult years. I also traveled the paths of my faith trek: from Jackson Avenue United Methodist Church in Memphis, Tennessee, to divinity school, to various pastorates, to my service at Brentwood United Methodist Church in Brentwood, Tennessee. In my mind I have reread books, listened again to speeches, and revisited people who strongly influenced my life.

This spiritual pilgrimage taught me several things. It taught me that I no longer need to prove anything to myself, to others, or to God. When we set out to prove ourselves, we usually wind up being a bit phony or defensive. Our honest desire to be the unique persons that God intended us to be frees us to be vulnerable in sharing our true selves with others.

In relation to being my true self, I also learned the value of being honest with how I feel. Leaders, be they political or pastoral, are often caught between saying what persons want to hear and what persons need to hear. If we put all our energy into giving persons what they want, we are merely calculating which way the wind is blowing. Jesus told his followers to merely say yes or no. I place great importance on speaking honestly and without guile.

On my journey, I discovered that I needed to sharpen my powers of theological perception and discernment. The church is not just another institution; it is a faith community under the governance of Christ seeking to edify believers and redeem the world.

I want to come to a deeper understanding of what God wants to do through the churches I serve. My discernment of what God is doing in the world requires my intentionality in prayer, disciplined study, and careful reflection. I find these actions necessary because shallow, unfounded theology is irrelevant to life's complexities. Those in pastoral leadership should always seek faithful discernment.

Taking a journey within myself was both a painful and a joyful experience. All in all, I enjoyed meeting myself on the winding roadways of my inner map.

It's worth pondering.

✦ FOR THE SAKE OF OTHERS

I believe that God manifests the divine self in three ways—as Creator, as Redeemer, and as Holy Spirit. Through the Holy Spirit, God is with us. Thus, God is not far removed and distant. Rather, God is near at hand and within us.

The Holy Spirit is not only with us but also actively working in our lives. It empowers us to live out the Christian way of life. Without the empowering presence of the Holy Spirit, we are like cars without engines. If we try to live without a dependence on the Holy Spirit, we will live only out of our own resources, and such living is not enough to get us through the tough times.

I also believe that there are certain evidences or signs of the Holy Spirit. The New Testament teaches that those who are open to the indwelling spirit of God bear certain fruit. The signs of the Spirit's presence are love, compassion, kindness, meekness, patience, forbearance, forgiveness, and discernment—to mention but a few. Those who acknowledge and live by the Spirit are those whose lives manifest the fruit of the Spirit.

The presence of the Holy Spirit is unattainable through hard work. Working toward a goal is one of the sure realities of life. We are meant to work for a living—work at our relationships, work at receiving a good education, work at outreach, work at reconciliation, work at achieving our goals. The Holy Spirit is not something that we work for in life; it comes to us as a gift. The Holy Spirit is God's freely given gift.

But here is the catch: God does not give us the Holy Spirit for ourselves alone. If we experience God as Holy Spirit, we experience God not only for ourselves but also for others. Above all else, the Holy Spirit is given to the church for the sake of others.

It's worth pondering,

⭐ GOOD TO BE WRONG

Something in me wants to be right—I want to have the right answer, and I want to make the right decisions.

Perhaps I should not admit to it in print, but I am wrong more times than I can count. These instances make me unhappy, hurt my inflated ego, and bruise my pride.

But I must admit that it is, at times, good to be wrong.

In the ninth grade I wanted to make the Treadwell High School basketball team. I practiced, dreamed, planned, and did everything in my power to make the final cut. However, it was not to be. Since I did not make the squad, the only available course was Miss Cooley's speech class. Because of that class, I began participating in debate, acting, and competitive speech. Now, as I look back across those years, I am glad that I was wrong about basketball.

As a student pastor, I wanted to be sent to a particular church circuit. Much to my chagrin, I was sent to Enville. Had it worked out another way I would have missed knowing the unpretentious, down-to-earth people in the Enville community.

Prior to our having children, I thought that I would like to be the father of a girl and a boy. Instead, I was blessed with two wonderful daughters, and it was good to be wrong.

I was wrong about needing pews in the balcony in a church I served. I honestly thought that we would not need the balcony seating, except perhaps for Christmas Eve and Easter services. Little did I know that our worship attendance would increase by a few hundred congregants in the span of a couple of years. It was good to be wrong.

Thirty years ago, I sincerely held to some beliefs that I no longer believe to be true. My mind has changed. I am now pleased to discover that I was wrong.

Life takes many funny turns. It is good that many of the turns are not of our own making. Often it is a grand relief to be wrong.

It's worth pondering.

SURRENDER IS NOT A DIRTY WORD

Victory is a positive word; surrender is not. Surrender is waving the white flag. Surrender is what we are taught not to do. We are to shun and avoid it at all cost. Winning is the ultimate goal.

But, in my opinion, surrender is an action that all of us take. All of us, every single one of us, will surrender our lives to someone or some thing. At times we give our lives to that which is bad. On other occasions we surrender our souls to that which is good.

Most of the time we will surrender to something that we perceive as being bigger or more powerful. Unconsciously, we allow ourselves to give in to that which promises to give us something in return.

So we surrender to work, to our families, to ideas or concepts, to drugs, to relationships, to just about anything. Surrender may not be a conscious choice. Gradually, and over long periods of time, we drift into many forms of surrender.

I believe that we should be aware of that to which we surrender ourselves. Giving in to false gods can lead to an unfulfilled life. Surrendering to the God of Jesus Christ can bring the kind of joy that the world cannot give.

It's worth pondering.

✦ THE DEVIL OF THE NOONDAY SUN

What is the worst thing that can happen to a person? The death of a child? The death of a spouse or parent? The loss of a career or job? Facing rejection? Starvation? Addiction? I could make a pretty long list. But in my opinion, none of these is the worst thing that can happen.

Acedia, or what the desert fathers and mothers called "the devil of the noonday sun" is the worst thing a person can experience. *Acedia* is a spiritual boredom or indifference to matters of faith. It leads to a heart so hard that it cannot feel for others. It can drag a person so far down that one is unable to live by his or her own principles.

For people who once had faith, *acedia* is not something that happens suddenly. Rather, it slips up on us, often unawares. It comes on slowly like the silent creeping of night into the otherwise brightness of day. It shatters the soul, leaving only the shell of a person.

The danger of *acedia* is decreased when we faithfully keep the spiritual disciplines of worship, prayer, meditation, searching the scriptures, receiving the sacrament, and taking part in Christian fellowship.

It's worth pondering.

✦ A MATURE FAITH

The words *spirituality* and *spiritual growth* are on the lips of many persons today. And rightly so, because we each must take responsibility for our own spiritual lives. If we are to grow spiritually, here are some ideas to consider.

Life is a gift, not an entitlement. To see life as a gift is to stand in awe of life and rejoice in it. Life's greatest gift is God's gift in Jesus Christ. We are also endowed with unique gifts. These gifts are given for the benefit of others.

Those who grow spiritually are those who have a deep commitment to love—not just any kind of love, but an openness and a readiness to accept God and other people into one's heart.

Discernment is a critical part of spiritual growth. Discernment helps us thoroughly know ourselves and creates an awareness of our own sinfulness and of the amazing and forgiving love of God. To discern is to be penitential and joyful at the same time—penitential because we discern how far we have all fallen short of the glory of God; joyful because the glory still outshines our shortcomings.

Growing spiritually requires patience, and patience requires courage. It takes courage to be still and wait. Waiting can be difficult in our always busy culture. For us, "doing" is more important than "being." I find that waiting for God and God's timing is more important than trying to appear busy before the Lord.

Finally, if we are to grow spiritually, we must willingly embrace solitude so that we might become more available to what the Holy Spirit is doing in our hearts. We do not have yesterday, and we do not know about tomorrow; but if we intentionally participate in the "now," there is a greater possibility that we will experience the holy in the everyday activities of life.

A mature faith does not come quickly. It comes to us on the long, winding path of love, discernment, patience, and solitude. But it begins by truly believing that life is a gift.

It's worth pondering.

FORGIVENESS

⭐ SETTLING OUR DIFFERENCES

We try to settle our differences with one another in many ways. Some of us try to settle our differences by avoiding them, ignoring them, putting our heads in the sand like the proverbial ostrich.

Others of us try to handle our differences by fighting back. We clench our fists and set our jaws. We practice an eye-for-an-eye and a tooth-for-a-tooth ethics. We harbor grudges. We act out our resentments, and we believe that the punishment should equal the offense.

Matthew 5:17-26 speaks to us about two ways to handle our differences. The first is to learn to live by the ethics of a higher righteousness. According to this higher ethic, it is not only wrong to murder, it is also wrong to hate.

This passage also indicates another way for us to settle our differences. Matthew writes, "So when you are offering your gift at the altar, if you remember that your brother or sister has something against you, leave your gift there before the altar and go; first be reconciled to your brother or sister, and then come and offer your gift" (5:23-24). Being reconciled to one another is far more important than any gift we might leave at the altar.

Settling the differences that exist between persons is crucial. And such differences can be settled if we live by the higher righteousness and seek to be reconciled to one another. If we do not live by a higher standard and seek reconciliation, our differences will not go away. Instead, they will fester and grow until we are separated more and more from others, from ourselves, and, ultimately, from God.

It's worth pondering.

✦ LAW AND GOSPEL

As followers of Jesus Christ, we live with God's commandments and God's forgiveness. Our pride, overconfidence, and self-focus brings us face-to-face with Christ's commandments. The commandments are

"'Love your neighbor as yourself'" (Mark 12:31).

"'Do to others as you would have them do to you'" (Matt. 7:12).

"'Love the Lord your God with all your heart, and with all your soul, and with all your mind, and with all your strength'" (Mark 12:30).

"'First take the log out of your own eye, and then you will see clearly to take the speck out of your neighbor's eye'" (Luke 6:42).

Forgive "'[not] seven times, but, I tell you, seventy-seven times'" (Matt. 18:22).

Learning and living Christ's commandments keep us in right relationship with God and one another.

On the other hand, when we fail, sin, and hurt others, ourselves, or God, we need to experience Christ's loving forgiveness. We are human, and we all commit sins of omission and commission. Our thoughts, words, and deeds can separate us from God, each other, and ourselves. When we fail and are broken, we need to experience God's healing love.

As Christians, we proclaim and live out both the commandments of Christ (law) and the love of Christ (gospel). Law without gospel can lead to harsh legalism. Gospel without law can become permissive. Neither the commandments nor the love of Christ were defeated by the Cross.

It's worth pondering.

WHEN LIFE DOESN'T COME OUT RIGHT

One Friday morning I served Holy Communion to ninety-six members of my church's youth choir just before they boarded two buses for Texas. As the choir left the sanctuary, one of the parents said, "I hope everything comes out right."

Therein lies a desire that all of us have. We like for things to come out right. Whether we are building a bookcase or putting plumbing in an outdoor spigot, we like for everything to fit.

This notion started in our early childhood. One of our first toys was likely a set of blocks. With these blocks we learned a sense of order, a sense of rightness, a sense of fitting here and not fitting there. We like for things to come out right.

Yet the more we love order, the greater our frustration when we cannot make things fit as we think they should.

I've watched a child pound a stack of blocks with a wooden hammer because she could not make them stack up just right. We know how it is to come home and get along miserably with our family because things would not come out right at work.

Carry this a little further. We not only want our blocks to fit, we also want life to come out right—that is, right for us. And most of us are willing to pay a fantastic price to ensure that life comes out as we attempt to prearrange it. I know persons who have lived their entire lives in this way.

But wise people know that life does not always come out right. No matter how hard we try, life will not come out right—and in this we see the value of forgiveness.

It's worth pondering.

PRAYER

 WHY PRAY?

I do not understand all there is to know about prayer. It is not uncommon for prayer to seem like a game of hide-and-seek in which we are seeking and God is hiding. Yet, even in the moments when prayer seems fruitless, I cannot cease praying.

My need to draw near to God's presence brings me back to the act of prayer, and I believe that my seeking will prove more than worthwhile. Prayer is about having a shared life with God. It is a way of being present with God, and I am convicted that if I pray from my heart, I will find God.

Prayer opens our finite hearts and minds to an infinite God. Through prayer, we can experience the guidance of God who strengthens us in our search for truth, goodness, righteousness, and healing.

Prayer, spoken from the heart, has the power to bring us into the presence of God. We may not find the process easy—we may not feel God's presence all at once or every time we pray—but I have found that God appears when I least expect it and in the most common of places.

It's worth pondering.

⭐ PRAYING FOR SINNERS

The sign in the front yard of the small, weather-beaten, rural church read, "Come Here Where Sinners Are Prayed For." I saw the sign as I drove on a remote section of Georgia highway on the way to Atlanta.

While staying in an Atlanta motel, I thumbed through the phone book looking for the address of a particular congregation. Located in the middle of one of those pages was an advertisement inviting people to an affluent church that offered a "Complete Recreational Program."

One church presented itself as being concerned about sinners, while the other congregation invited people to come for recreation.

In my opinion the plain one-room church had a clearer understanding of what it means to be the body of Christ than the congregation that could afford to put a big advertisement in the phone book.

My concern is that in the modern church it can be easier to experience recreation than to find times and places where "sinners are prayed for." We sin each and every time we fail to live in the fullness of Christ. Sin is any thought, word, or deed that causes us to fall short of who God wants us to be. This means that all of us are sinners. And all of us and all people everywhere need to be "prayed for."

It's worth pondering.

⭐ TOUCHDOWN PRAYERS

In the past few years, news outlets have reported stories of football players who kneel in the end zone after scoring a touchdown. According to some published reports, these players are merely thanking God for having the athletic ability to score points.

I am not one to question the motives or the theology of those who kneel in prayer at a football game, but something about this ritual causes me to reflect. Why is it that players do not drop on one knee after a player has been injured? Why do they not offer a prayer of thanksgiving for a substitute player who makes his first tackle in the first game in which he has ever played? Why do they not pray a prayer for forgiveness after an outpouring of profanity? Or why is there no prayer of sympathy and compassion for the disappointment of the losing team? Should public demonstrations of prayer only be for those times when points are scored?

One of the central teachings of the Christian faith is that we pray for others first and ourselves last. Praying only after a winning touchdown reverses the natural order of prayer. We may thank God for an accomplishment, while forgetting to hold before God the hurts and hopes of others.

Praying after a touchdown says more about the church's failure to teach the meaning of prayer than it does about athletes who are merely being true to their understanding. Let us pray that the church will teach all of us how to pray.

It's worth pondering.

WORSHIP

✴ OFFERING OURSELVES

It is not unusual for me to hear congregants say, "Sometimes I don't get anything from church." I know what they mean by this statement, but there is another side to that coin. When we go to an athletic event, we are supposed to get something out of it. When we read a book or go to the theater, we rightly expect to get some pleasure out of it. When we are involved in an educational endeavor, we expect to gain knowledge. We approach many activities with the primary motive of gleaning something from them.

In my opinion, the primary—though not the only—reason for going to public worship is not what we receive from it but what we give to God through the experience. In corporate worship, what we give to God is more important than what we get.

Through worship we declare God's worthiness to be praised. In worship we give our attention to God through song, prayer, and the reading and hearing of God's word. Through baptism, we give our children over to the church. Through funerals, we commend our loved ones to God's eternal care. Through marriage, we give ourselves to each other and to Christ. Through the Lord's Supper, we give ourselves over to the sacrament. Sunday morning worship is not about getting; it is about giving God our adoration and praise.

If we come to the church expecting to receive entertainment, we are setting ourselves up to be disappointed. When we come to worship focused on what we can reverently give to Christ, we are opening ourselves up to that which is holy. And by giving our attention to God, we find ourselves receiving more than we ever expected.

It's worth pondering.

⭐ A WORLD SHORN OF GOD

Will we be formed by the living Christ, or will we be formed by the forces of culture? The powers of our culture are very strong. Money, sex, television, and entertainment have the muscle to shape us. Their message is clear and convincing:

- Achievement and status are more important than beliefs
- The deepest needs of life will be satisfied if one worships sex, power, and money
- Accepting guidance from anyone is a sign of weakness
- Power is to be determined not by service but by success
- Hope is to be found in the doctrine of more, and not in the power of love
- Winning is better than learning from the defeats of life
- Peace and tranquility are more important than the strength that comes from struggle

I have decided that the forces that drive the unseen powers of culture do not care about us. They do not love us. They do not will the best for us. These principalities and powers, as Paul called them, want to exploit us and hold us captive. They want us to serve them.

One day, Jesus told a story about a person who built a house upon a rock. When the rain fell and the wind blew, the house did not fall. Jesus also told about a person who built a house upon the sand. When the storms of life came, the house did not stand.

If we do not build the house of our lives on solid foundations, our culture will shape us from a world shorn of God. Why do we worship the gods of our culture instead of our loving God?

It's worth pondering.

 GETTING OUR BEARINGS

I like to attend church when I am on vacation. Not only do I feel a need for the discipline of Sunday worship, I also enjoy experiencing worship in various settings.

One church service that I attended while on vacation will forever be stamped on my memory. The service was reverent, warm, and inviting. The sermon was well-prepared and beautifully delivered. In fact, I found myself thinking about it for the following weeks!

Immediately after the service a man spoke to me, told me his name, and invited me to join him for refreshments that were being served in a nearby hall. During our conversation he asked, "Do you attend worship with regularity?"

"Yes, I go three times every Sunday morning, forty-nine Sundays out of the year." He looked puzzled.

"Three different congregations or just one?"

"Just one," I replied.

"Do you hear three different sermons?"

"Same one," I said.

"The preacher must really be a good one," he replied.

"Some days he's a lot better than others," I said.

Finally he caught on and said, "You must be clergy!"

"Yes," I replied, "And I truly appreciated being in your worship service today. It was most inspiring."

Then the man said, "I come every Sunday. Helps me get my bearings. I would not miss coming to worship for anything. Every Sunday, without fail, something speaks to me. I've failed this church a lot of times, but this congregation has never failed me."

I never tire of visiting new churches and seeing the ways in which God is praised. And luckily for me, most of the churches I visit know how to welcome a stranger. In so doing, they follow the example of Jesus who recognized, received, and honored the stranger. Allowing myself the opportunity to be a welcomed stranger reminds me of the importance of welcoming others.

It's worth pondering.

★ HONORING GOD

In Paul's letter to Corinth, he encourages the church there to, "Honor God with your bodies" (1 Cor. 6:20, NIV).

We find this hard to hear because we know how to adorn the body, but we do not know how to glorify God with the body.

Recently I bought a storage container for my closet. As I set myself to the task of organizing, I happened to look at all my clothing—trousers, shirts, suits, sport coats, and topcoats. Most of my clothing is there not because I need it, but because I need to glorify my body.

A lot of the physical fitness craze today is not as much about health as it is about glorifying the body. Television commercials try to sell us new exercise regimens, diet foods and drinks, and workout clothing. To be sure, it is important to stay in shape, but much of this craze is just to glorify the body.

But the apostle Paul corrected that notion when he said, "Honor God with your bodies." So, how can we honor God with our bodies?

We honor God with the body when we physically do things that glorify God. Or, in other words, we honor God with the body when we allow our bodies to be used in service to humankind. This is probably the greatest glorification of God with the body. It is bodily involvement in Christianity that really matters.

The wonderful thing is that anybody can glorify God with the body. The culture in which we live says that only beautiful bodies are worth anything. Our faith says that every body can glorify God.

It's worth pondering.

 WORSHIPING TOGETHER

Every now and then someone will write an article in a magazine or newspaper on why people attend church. The article is usually based on some survey that has been conducted by a secular outfit. The answers are usually as weak as water: "I want my children to learn Bible stories"; "I like the pastor—he preaches down-to-earth sermons"; "Our church is friendly, and we need community"; "We love good music;" and so on.

Rarely does anyone respond, "To worship God." Plain and simple. Straightforward. That is the reason we come to church. Believers assemble to worship because God has called them together.

In worship, the community of God's people meet to hear God's word spoken in scripture, sermon, sacrament, music, and liturgy. Sometimes it is done well; other times it is done poorly. But through it all, that which is proclaimed and acted out in worship creates faith. And through that faith, the community responds with praise, obedience, and commitment.

Participating year after year in corporate worship in which scripture is central prevents God's people from creating a religion that's grown out of some private notion about God. The discipline of common worship enables faith to be passed from person to person.

Every now and then I hear someone say something like, "I can worship God on the golf course, on the lake, or while walking by a mountain stream." I agree because I have worshiped God in those places. But not on Sunday morning. If every believer went his or her separate way to pursue his or her own activity, where would the word be read and proclaimed? Where would faith be formed and handed down from one generation to another?

Being Christian is about being part of a community of those who trust the promises that God made in Christ.

It's worth pondering.

SIN
★ ★

 SIN IS . . .

I cannot adequately speak about sin without first speaking about what it means to live under the dominion of God. As persons of faith, we are intended to live by the love commandment of Jesus. If faith is to be consciously lived as if love rules our lives, then sin means that something other than God has dominion over our life.

When we do not allow the divine to rule, we are selfishly directed toward ourselves. Such self-direction leads to egocentricity, which is opposite to the divine will and, therefore, sin. Whenever egocentricity rules, our fellowship with God is destroyed and divine love does not and cannot rule, which is one way to look at the nature of sin.

In 1 Corinthians 13:5, Paul tells us that the characteristic of divine love is that it "does not insist on its own way," which is the exact opposite of sin. The essence of sin is seen when our life is focused on seeking our own way.

This seeking of our own way appears in many forms. It can even appear in our seeking after God, if such seeking attempts to secure something for our own benefit by divine help. When we use God to fill our egocentric needs, sin is present in its most sublimated and deceptive form. Sin is practiced when we do not live under the dominion of God's love and when we try to make God the servant of our human desires and purposes.

If sin is insisting on our own way instead of living under the dominion of God, Paul was right on target when he said, "I do not do the good I want, but the evil I do not want is what I do. Now if I do what I do not want, it is no longer I that do it, but sin that dwells within me" (Rom. 7:19-20). We are so mired in sin that we cannot extricate ourselves from its hold. Only God can deliver us and free us, and that is where we need to place our trust. Thus, faith in the grace of God redeems us. Human effort will not do it. Only trust in God's love will set us free from sin.

It's worth pondering.

★ WORTH AND WINNING

We are not the creators of the order in which we live. That Creator built a pattern of righteousness in the world that cannot be ignored. If we persist in breaking the laws of the universe, we will break against them. If we go against God's intended pattern, we will get splinters.

A generation ago Grantland Rice said it's "not that you won or lost—but how you played the Game." However, the philosophy of Grantland Rice has now been supplanted by another dictum: Vince Lombardi's words, "Winning isn't everything; it's the only thing."

Many of our problems today grow out of the Lombardi "theology." Winning is an obsession in our culture. Because of this, persons are more willing to bend and break rules to secure the goal.

A few years ago the World Football League distorted attendance figures in order to seem more successful than it was. Congregations often get obsessed with attendance figures, not because individual souls are cared about, but because there is a need to prove success by posting growing numbers. Individuals will magnify income as a way of proving they are winners. Companies will show a false bottom line because of the need to be in the winners' circle.

Let us not forget that the Christian gospel tells us that our final worth as persons is not determined by how we come out in this or that competitive race. Our worth is determined by the content of our character, our service to others, and our desire to love God and neighbor.

We rightly admire those who achieve and accomplish, but we should never let the "wins" of others draw us into winning at any price.

It's worth pondering.

SIN AND GOD'S FORGIVENESS

Have you ever found yourself walking on the beach looking for the perfect shell? Imagine yourself walking the shoreline. Feel the damp sand on your bare feet and the sea breeze blowing through your hair. You scan your eyes from the rolling sea back to the shore. But the only shells you find are either broken or blemished, so you toss them back into the water.

If we are honest with ourselves, we live with the knowledge that our lives are broken or tarnished in some way, not unlike the shells we find at the ocean's shore. Some of us are broken by the roaring waves of life. Others are broken by moral failure. The tide of sin has often compromised our highest values.

Orthodox Christian teachings say that we do not have the power to repair ourselves, but we do have the strength to open ourselves to Christ Jesus who will, through the Holy Spirit, grant us forgiveness and restoration. Unlike those of us who have thrown the broken shells back into the ocean, the God of Jesus does not ask for perfection.

The church, as the bride of Christ, understands itself as a community of forgiven people who offer forgiveness to others. The noble purpose of the church is to reconcile persons to God and to one another by the example set by Christ.

We all sin, and yet God's forgiveness is abundant and available to us all.

It's worth pondering.

FEAR

 ANXIETY

Someone once said to me, "The curse of anxiety is that it takes itself too seriously." Truly none of us will escape having a firsthand experience with anxiety. None of us will always live in the golden days of independence, prosperity, and success.

Various seeds can produce the plant of anxiety.

Anxiety arises out of a sense of loss. Loss of a significant relationship or job or location can be the source of great anxiety.

Anxiety also comes from feeling trapped—trapped by a relationship or an addiction or a career or circumstances beyond our control.

Those who feel stifled creatively often feel anxious. When peace is attained through creative outlets, anxiety may rise when no outlets can be found.

Anxiety may overtake us when our resources to cope with life are no longer adequate defenses.

If we are to handle our anxieties we must first face them. Put a label on them. Call them by a name. Acknowledge their power. That's the first step.

Wise persons know the importance of putting themselves in the hands of friends, pastors, counselors, and professional caregivers.

Anyone who has walked the road of anxiety knows that the more anxieties are denied, the bigger they become.

First Peter 5:7 encourages us to handle our anxieties by casting them on the Lord. It sounds simple, but there is great truth in this advice. When we cast our burdens upon the Lord, we acknowledge the spiritual resources that are far greater than our resources. Countless persons with anxiety have turned to the vast pool of spiritual resources—prayer, Bible study, worship, partaking of the sacraments, contemplation—and found significant assistance.

When we cast our burdens upon the Lord, we concern ourselves with how God wants our lives to be and not how we want them to be. As believers, we know that God is with us as we face, work through, and rise above anxieties.

It's worth pondering.

TRUSTING OUR REGRETS TO GOD

I cannot remember how many times I have placed my hands on a casket and said, "For as much as the departed has entered into life immortal, we, therefore, commit his (or her) body to its final resting place, remembering how Jesus said upon the cross, 'Father, into your hands I commend my spirit'" (Luke 23:46).

Though I have stood by many coffins and have prayed with a large number of dying persons, I am not able to put myself in the position of those who are about to depart this life. Could it be that we bear more than pain and sorrow when we are departing this life?

I expect that one of the heaviest burdens for a dying person is regret. Regret about conflicts unresolved. Regret about breached relationships not healed. Regret about potential unfulfilled. Regret about promises not kept and years that will never be lived. When we come to the time of transition to the next life, there will be unfinished business.

The greater our purpose, the more we love others, the more we savor the goodness of everyday life, the more life has been an adventure—the more we will regret. We will regret not having more of what we highly treasured.

When I come to my own dying moments, I hope I can trust my regrets to God's care and mercy. What other choice do I have?

It's worth pondering.

PREACHING

★ ★

JUST THE BISCUITS

Aside from pancakes, popcorn, and scrambled eggs, I have never cooked anything worth writing home about. I remember when my wife's Sunday school class hosted a Valentine's dinner for which the husbands were required to prepare and bring a dish. Since I could not take pancakes, popcorn, or scrambled eggs, I was in a bind.

Realizing my plight, Janene dug in her recipe box, pulled out an index card, and said, "Maybe you can make this. It's easy."

The recipe that she handed me was for a dessert called "Preacher's Coming"—one of those delightful desserts that calls for an abundance of chocolate, nuts, butter, sugar, and vanilla ice cream.

At first I was a bit confused. Her recipe called for "conf. sugar," so I asked if we had any "confederate sugar." It called for crushed vanilla wafers, so I broke the wafers using my hands instead of the blender. It called for butter, and I used margarine. It called for a sprinkling of pecans, and I used an entire bag.

After working four times as long as the recipe was supposed to take, I finished my project and put it in the freezer. When the evening arrived, the dishes were spread on the table for judging. The women went from dish to dish, tasting and comparing to determine which recipe would take home the prize. After sampling all of the fare, the women voted and chose a winner.

You could have knocked me over with a feather when I was awarded a set of measuring spoons for having made the winning dessert. I won, even though I could not read the recipe, could not get the measurements straight, and could not properly identify the ingredients.

Just goes to show you that we often succeed in spite of our mistakes. It was the taste, not the recipe, that ultimately mattered.

I often discuss the art of sermon preparation with a good friend of mine. He is fond of saying, "Joe, when you preach, always give your congregation the biscuits and never the recipe. They do not care about what's in the recipe. All they want is something to chew on."

It's worth pondering.

★ THINK WITH YOUR HEART

One day a student of mine at Vanderbilt Divinity School asked, "What is the best church you ever served?" It was a difficult question to answer, but I said that Enville United Methodist Church would be near the top of the list.

I served Enville while I was a divinity school student from 1961–1964. The town of Enville is located in rural West Tennessee, not very far from the Tennessee River. The congregants were farmers, home-makers, store owners, cotton gin operators, and factory workers. About seventy-five persons made up the membership of the congregation.

The believers of Enville had a wisdom that touched both the head and the heart. This wisdom came from living with a daily dependence on the land and one another. The members of the church formed a lov-ing and tight-knit community.

In the early days of my ministry at Enville, my sermons sounded too much like the teachings of my professors at divinity school. I was constantly weaving into my sermons what I had heard my teachers say, but I wasn't reaching the congregation.

After one Sunday service, a church member offered sound advice while we were sitting around her dinner table. She said, "Joe, when you are preparing sermons, think with your heart." It stuck. She did not need to say another word. Even now I can hear her say, "Think with your heart."

To think with your heart does not diminish the need to do informed thinking, to think deeply, and to reflect theologically on the meaning of life. When we let our heart interact with our mind we are better prepared to speak the truth in love. When heart and mind join, we are better able to understand what love requires.

It's worth pondering.

GRACE THAT CHANGES

As a preacher of the gospel I bear a great responsibility for the souls of the congregation I serve. This responsibility keeps me occupied mentally, emotionally, and spiritually.

I want the gospel that I preach to both interpret life and alter life. Interpreting life from the vantage point of the Christian faith is a significant part of my task. But I must go further. I need to proclaim the gospel in a way alters the character of life.

My goal is not to preach a kind of grace that saves us without changing us. Emphasis on saving grace alone eases our consciences without changing the basic character of our lives. A gospel that does not change us does not require fairness toward others, nor does it call us to be more loving.

If a grace that changes us is so important, how do we know that we are being changed? If divine love is actively working to restore the image of God in us, we are being changed. We know that we are being changed if we are growing in our imitation of God's love.

I pray that my teachings result not only in the interpretation of life, but also in the changing of life.

It's worth pondering.

ADVENT
and
CHRISTMAS

⭐ WAITING AND LOOKING

As a child I remember that the most difficult part of Christmas was simply waiting for it to arrive. The distance between Thanksgiving and Christmas Day seemed more like an eternity than a month. Days seemed like weeks. Weeks felt like months. Time seemed to stand still.

Waiting is foreign to those of us who are accustomed to moving in the fast lane. Waiting seems unnatural. Knowing how to wait is, at best, an uncommon trait. We hunger for immediate satisfaction, and the idea of delayed gratification is a stranger to our thinking.

Our society is alive with the symbols of our unwillingness or inability to wait. Exquisite taste does not sell frozen dinners; the ease in which they are prepared is what makes this fare popular. Similarly, we might choose to dine at a fast-food chain instead of a formal restaurant to save time. A leisurely meal and good conversation are sacrificed for fast service and the check—and all because of busy schedules.

When we wait, we live in the in-between. Waiting is like knowing but not knowing, and it is how we wait that matters. Some will wait with an impatience, a tapping foot. Others will wait with anticipation, eagerly looking for Christ's coming in a variety of places—in the quiet visit of an old friend, in the reading of scripture, or in the symbols of congregational worship.

Knowing how to wait and where to look are the preludes to the Messiah's birth.

It's worth pondering.

✦ A CHRISTMAS SPIRIT

I heard it said more than once this year. In fact, I heard it over and over again. People said, "I don't have the Christmas spirit this year," and "It just doesn't feel like Christmas."

What do those statements mean? Is there some kind of "feeling" during the holiday season that we do not experience during the other eleven months? Or is there a certain "spirit" that dies on December twenty-sixth and does not resurface until the next year? Is the "Christmas spirit" something that can be created with music, lights, glitter, and special effects? Is it a feeling that we experienced in a time gone by and hunger to recapture?

And if there is a Christmas spirit, where can we find it? In the bustling aisles of a department store? On a TV Christmas special? While baking favorite goodies for family and friends? Perhaps it can be found while taking Holy Communion or while lighting the Christ candle on Christmas Eve.

Because many people know about the Christmas spirit but never experience what they think it is or should be, there is often great disappointment when December twenty-fifth comes and goes.

One December morning, I went to a local nursery to purchase a poinsettia for my wife. The nursery was tastefully decorated with ribbons, greenery, and oversized bows. Hot cider and cookies were being served to all of the customers. Beautiful evergreens were available for purchase. A delightful fragrance was in the air. The cashier was totaling one sale after the next.

As I approached a salesperson I asked, "Are things going well?" Without blinking she replied, "Christmas is a horror story; there is no other way to express it. And I, for one, will be glad when it is over." Her harsh words took some of the joy out of my floral gift.

If I am honest, there are times when I have felt like that salesperson. Leading a congregation through Advent and Christmas is no easy task. Details are stacked upon details. All that must go into the four Sundays of Advent and the three services on Christmas Eve is enough to create mild stress, if not sheer panic. But I understand that what I do contributes to the experience of those around me. I look for every opportunity during the Advent season to point beyond the mundane details to that which is holy. For me, that's the real Christmas spirit.

It's worth pondering.

✦ BELIEVING TOGETHER

Next to the infant Jesus, Mary is one of the central characters in the stories about the birth of the Messiah. Our image of Mary has been shaped by Christmas cards and pageants that depict her humbly looking into the manger at her newborn child. The Gospel of Luke portrays her as a model of obedience, displaying such virtues as patience, gentleness, and attentiveness.

Rarely do we reflect on how Mary felt when she discovered that she had conceived and would bear a son. Luke says that she was perplexed, afraid, and full of questions about how such a thing could be true. In her first appearance in Luke's Gospel, she is not a calm, strong, young woman of faith. In the beginning she cannot sing. She can only question in her heart. She is afraid.

Having heard the message that she will be the mother of the one who will be called the Son of God, Mary visits her cousin Elizabeth. When Mary arrives at her cousin's house, Elizabeth confirms what God is doing in Mary's life. Elizabeth interprets for Mary, confirms for Mary, and helps Mary understand God's action in her life.

Elizabeth says to Mary, "Blessed are you among women, and blessed is the fruit of your womb. . . . And blessed is she who believed that there would be a fulfillment of what was spoken to her by the Lord" (Luke 1:42, 45). Elizabeth helps Mary see what God is doing in her life. It is worth noting that Mary sings the "Magnificat" not before, but after Elizabeth helps her see and understand what God is doing through her.

On our own, we may find it difficult to believe in the fulfillment of God's promises. But in coming together like Mary and Elizabeth, we can depend on our brothers and sisters to support our faith and belief that God's promises are with us, for us, and through us. At times, we need others to help us understand.

It's worth pondering.

 JOSEPH

Joseph is in a bind! Mary, his betrothed, is pregnant. Both law and custom are on his side. Joseph can break the engagement, thereby putting Mary to shame and leaving her in an untenable position. Or he can charge her with infidelity, thus repudiating her and reducing her to a life of shame.

While Joseph is trying to decide what to do, an angel of the Lord appears to him in a dream and says, "Joseph, Son of David, do not be afraid to take Mary as your wife, for that conceived in her is from the Holy Spirit. She will bear a son, and you are to name him Jesus, for he will save his people from their sins" (Matt. 1:20-21).

According to the customs and standards of his day, Joseph has every right to end his engagement to Mary. With law and tradition backing him up, not one person in the village of Nazareth will argue with him. He can slip easily out of a most difficult situation.

But instead of taking the easy way out, Joseph heeds the angel's command and takes Mary as his wife. Instead of separating himself from Mary, Joseph loves her and cares for her. For Joseph, compassion is more important than conventional expectations. Love, justice, and a sense of responsibility are more important than tradition and law.

The biblical story of Joseph makes the heart grow soft because Joseph is true to his understanding of what God expects of him. He does as God commands even though law, tradition, and custom give him permission to take a road much wider and much less difficult. Instead of taking the wide path, Joseph chooses to trust God.

Joseph does as the angel requests, naming his son Jesus, a Greek form of the Hebrew "Joshua," meaning "he shall save." As the ancient Israelites saved their people from foreign oppressors, so will Jesus save people from sin. How can we be like Joseph during the Advent season?

It's worth pondering.

 PRESENT AND FUTURE

For children, Christmas lies in the distant future; for adults, Christmas arrives far too quickly. For youngsters, the journey to Christmas is a long one; for grown-ups, Christmas is just around the corner. When I was a child, I thought December was the longest month of the entire year. I would use a calendar to mark off each passing day, hoping to hasten the coming of Christmas. The closer I got to Christmas, the farther away it seemed. Christmas Eve may well have lasted a week!

Now as an adult, the Christmas season rushes by. There seems to be too much to do in too little time. There are gifts to buy, meals to prepare, and families to entertain. The demands of Christmas seem all too immediate and arrive all too soon.

For children and adults, the coming of December twenty-fifth shapes their lives between the first Sunday in Advent and Christmas Day. It determines how they will live between "now" and "then."

In 1966 I was the associate pastor of St. Luke's United Methodist Church in Memphis, Tennessee. On a Thursday afternoon in the spring, the White House called to tell us that the vice president of the United States would be worshiping at St. Luke's Church the following Sunday morning. From Thursday afternoon until 10:50 a.m. Sunday morning, Mr. Humphrey's expected visit shaped our actions as a congregation. His coming determined how we would spend those few brief days. We knew that we must be ready for his arrival.

The earliest Christians earnestly believed that their lives were shaped by the second coming of Christ. They were convinced of their need to be ready for Christ's arrival, just as St. Luke's Church knew that it must be ready for the vice president's visit. This conviction was one of the towering marks of the early church.

If we believe that the Son of man is coming, then that belief will determine how we live in the present. But if we do not believe that the Son of Man is coming, we will shape the present like the past. Or we will shape the present as if nothing is about to happen.

I have a friend whose son is a student in a faraway college. This young freshman had not been home since he left in mid-August, but he was expected to return for Thanksgiving. Prior to his homecoming, his parents spent their energy getting ready for his arrival. For days, they anticipated the coming of their child. Preparations were made. His favorite foods were prepared. His room was cleaned. Members of the family planned to be home for his visit. The family members' actions had meaning and purpose because their present was being shaped by the future. Likewise, if we believe in the coming of the kingdom of God, then we will try to live every day in anticipation of that event.

But as we all know, preparing for a future event is arduous if we do not know when the event will occur. If we did not know when Christmas was coming, it would be hard to plan for that day. If we did not know when our son would be returning home from a long journey, it would be hard to prepare for his homecoming.

On the first Sunday of Advent, consider how you prepare for the God who came in Jesus Christ.

It's worth pondering.

THE MYSTERY OF THE SEASON

Few secular voices say anything profound about Christmas. Every now and then a voice will sound off about Christmas being too commercialized, and there is some truth to that.

We see commercialization in people spending money they do not have on presents that others neither need nor want. We see it in stores that pull out the Christmas decorations even before the Halloween pumpkins are put away. We see it in many of our children who know more about the legends of Rudolph, the Red-Nosed Reindeer, than about the stories of shepherds and magi. We see it in those who do not remember the one whose birth is honored on December twenty-fifth.

Yet, no matter how much we commercialize Advent and Christmas, we cannot destroy the mystery of the season. Beneath all of the hype and glitter lies a meaning that cannot be muffled or erased.

Though we cannot ruin it, neither can we fully understand the mystery of it all. We can come close to understanding the mystery, but we cannot fully comprehend it. Try as we might, our finite minds cannot grasp the infinite mystery that the God of creation came to earth as an innocent child. The mystery of it all defies our grandest imagination. Even music, scripture, and liturgy cannot completely disclose the mystery of the Incarnation.

I once read a newspaper column that suggested that Christmas ought to bring out our emotions, put a lump in our throats. Surely there is more to Christmas than a lump in the throat; more than a warm, sentimental feeling that bathes across our being; more than a warmth that is not experienced at any other time of the year. In our attempt to reduce the mystery of the season to some kind of concept or feeling that we can understand and experience, may we not forget that Christmas is about what God has done to save humankind.

It's worth pondering.

✦ NOT ABOUT WHAT WE DO

Too much emphasis is put on what we do to prepare for Christmas. Putting up decorations. Selecting and buying gifts. Trimming a tree. Attending parties. Preparing for houseguests. Arranging schedules with relatives. Responding to the expectations of others. All of these preparations have their place as we observe the holiday season, but, at a deeper level, Christmas is not about what we do. Christmas is about what God has done by coming to us in the innocence and vulnerability of a baby. In the infant, God does not overpower or force us to believe.

On Christmas Eve night, families will gather in a crowded church and sit elbow to elbow. The faithful and the unfaithful will sit side by side. Some will look with a blank stare. Others will be wide-eyed and wondering at the mystery of it all.

Even the most doubtful will understand that Christmas is a way of talking about what God has done. It is a way of speaking about God as Emmanuel, God with us.

If we focus too much on what we do instead of what God has done and is doing, we will have the experience and miss the meaning.

It's worth pondering.

 WAS AND IS

During Advent, I notice that we speak of the "was-ness" of the season—the way life was in times gone by. The was-ness of places like Nazareth and Bethlehem. The was-ness of Mary, Joseph, the shepherds, the magi, the innkeepers, the angelic choirs, and an infant's birth. The was-ness of past Christmases celebrated as a family or as a church.

I remember the Christmas pageants of my childhood—bedsheets for robes, towels for turbans, an apple crate for a manger. Whatever we could find for the building of a set. One year, I recited the entire chapter of Luke for the members of Jackson Avenue United Methodist Church in Memphis, Tennessee. These memories and many more represent the was-ness of the Christmas season.

But I also experience an "is-ness" about this season of the year. In spite of all of the glitz, commercialism, and hype, I know that Advent is a time of preparation for the observance of Christ's birth.

God wants to be among us—wants to come near us; wants to forgive us; wants to illumine the dark places in our lives; wants to fill us with love, joy, and peace. But God will not push God's presence on us—will not intrude, will not overpower, will not make us open our hearts. God comes to those who open themselves. If we are unwilling to grant God access to our darkness, God can do nothing. Whatever is acknowledged, God can take over. What God is not given cannot be taken away. The brokenness that is not presented to God cannot be repaired. But if we place our sins before God, we will be forgiven, breaking the power of those sins over us. That, in my opinion, is the "is-ness" of Advent.

It's worth pondering.

LENT

and

EASTER

⭐ HOPE, NOT WISH

Easter is often called the season of great hope. Some philosophers believe that what we call hope is in fact a form of wish-fulfillment thinking. How many of us find our life filled with wishes?

A child wishes for a bicycle; a student wishes for a car, a house, and a job. A sick person wishes to be cured; a poor man wishes for money; a prisoner wishes for freedom.

Wish-fulfillment thinking is like waiting for Santa Claus, whose task it is to satisfy very specific needs and desires. When our lives are filled with these types of specific concrete wishes, we are in constant danger of becoming disappointed, bitter, angry, or indifferent because some of our wishes won't come true. When that happens, we begin to feel betrayed.

Easter speaks to us about a hope that is more powerful than wishing. The hope of Easter is directed toward a God who can bring life from death. At the resurrection, the community comes to life again; the scattered are reassembled; the disillusioned find faith; the frightened become fearless; and those who denied and deserted are forgiven. We find the hope of Easter in God's promise to bring about a new creation.

Christian hope is, therefore, more than wish fulfillment. We "wish that," but we "hope in." Therein lies the difference.

It's worth pondering.

 GIVING UP TO TAKE ON

I have been taught that persons should give up something for Lent. Giving up something is a way of practicing self-denial and reminding ourselves of Jesus' sacrifice. Doing without is no virtue in and of itself. We can give up almost anything and remain as we have always been. However, if we give up something as a reminder of our Lord's passion, that act of giving up can become a helpful spiritual discipline.

But there is another side to the coin—a side that is not often mentioned. The other side is to also *take on* something for Lent, as a way of reminding ourselves that Christ took on the cross of love for us.

We could take on regular involvement in outreach, speaking out for justice and against injustice, prayerfully caring for our bodies, reading and studying the scripture daily, praying privately each day, attending weekly worship, obeying the prompting of the Holy Spirit, or being intentionally involved in advancing the cause of Christ.

Our lives include both giving up and taking on.

It's worth pondering.

THE RHYTHMS OF LIFE

Busy. This word characterizes much of our frenzied activity and life as a community. We are incredibly busy people. We move from task to task, person to person, mountain to mountain, opportunity to opportunity. We are driven, ambitious, motivated, and exhausted. Yet, in the midst of all of this busyness, life lacks a certain rhythm.

There needs to be a time of sabbath in all our lives, a time set aside from the harried and hurried side of life. This type of sabbath time includes four parts.

First, a sabbath requires a time for ceasing. We set aside time to quit what we are doing, to stop, to draw the line, to refuse to do any more. When we allow ourselves a moment of stillness, we can usually resume our tasks with more vigor, resourcefulness, and creativity.

Second, a sabbath requires a time for resting. We can relax, let go of to-do lists, and get in touch with the questions of our souls. Resting is not easy for many of us because we are active, and we place far greater value on working than on resting. Yet resting brings with it a certain amount of restoration, which can be healing to our spirits.

Third, a sabbath requires a time of embracing. By embracing, I mean clinging to the religious traditions and values given to us by the generations that have gone before. For example, reading scripture or a classic piece of literature or a biography of a great person of the past or merely stopping and being aware of our own heritage. If we do not embrace that which has gone before us, our lives can become rudderless, and we will unknowingly repeat the mistakes of the past.

Fourth, a sabbath requires a time of feasting. Feasting with family, friends, and significant others brings a special joy. Sitting around a table, holding hands, and telling stories feeds the spirit. Feasting is about more than eating; it's about talking and listening, planning and dreaming, forgiving and loving.

In these busy times we need more holy rhythms in our lives. We need times when our spirits can be held, nurtured, and supported. Not only will these holy rhythms make us more compassionate, they will also make us more courageous and more visionary.

During the season of Lent, we enter a time of repentance and preparation for the crucifixion and resurrection of Jesus Christ. As we think about what we will give up for Lent, let us also think about taking on some holy rhythms that bring restoration and direction.

It's worth pondering.

✦ BUSY WHITTLIN'

Back when I was a rural pastor, I enjoyed "going to town," as we called it. The small town of Enville, Tennessee, is a scant fifteen miles from Henderson, the county seat. It is not a long drive, but the village of two hundred people felt a long way from the "going to town" city.

Henderson boasts amenities that Enville would never have—a college, a hospital, a high school, restaurants, a jail, and a courthouse.

The courthouse benches, both inside and out, were more often than not filled with men who either played checkers or whittled. You could barely see the red and black squares on the checkerboard from almost constant use. Since the regulation checkers had long since been lost or broken, bottle tops were called into service. Coke bottle tops served as red checkers while root beer tops served as black.

Pop Guin was the undisputed checker champion. Every now and then someone would beat him, but not often. And when someone did edge out ol' Pop, it was big news all over town. Over the years Pop became the most well-known character in the county. He knew how to play checkers, and he would take on anybody who was big enough to see over the board.

The whittlers were also an interesting bunch. They came to the benches early and stayed late. You'd see the same familiar faces day in and day out. The same pile of shavings, the same knives, and the same benches. A few of the men were known as "drivers." They drove their wives to work at the shirt factory and then drove them home in the afternoon, after having whittled and played checkers all day. A good friend often observed that the whittlers whittled, but they "never made anything." He also said that the checker players were "entertaining themselves to death."

And that is a danger for all of us. Like those men at the courthouse, we are in danger of whittling away at life and not making anything. Life becomes nothing more than getting by—working the same job day in and day out, waiting for the weekend, paying bills, and giving enough away to salve our consciences. We can easily drift through life and not make anything or be involved in some cause that will outlive us.

There is also the danger of entertaining ourselves to death. I am saddened by the hordes of people who cannot be involved in worship, mission, and outreach because they have given entertainment a top priority. I often hear, "I can't come to worship because I have a tennis match," or "I can't attend a committee meeting because that's my bridge night," or "We can't be involved in a group for Bible study because our calendar is already full."

The season of Lent tells us that there is more to life than whittling and playing checkers. Lent speaks to us about the abundant life that can come from following the way of Christ. Jesus, as we know from the New Testament, identified with the pains and pressures of people. He gave himself to God and for others. He has shown us that the ultimate joy comes from sacrificing ourselves for others.

We are not hard-pressed to find opportunities to give ourselves to others. Such opportunities come every day. They meet us around every corner. Hurts and hopes come dressed in those very persons whose eyes and hearts are opened toward us.

The tragedy is that we might be so busy whittling and playing checkers that we would miss experiencing Christ when he comes dressed in the garb of another person's need.

It's worth pondering.

LOVE STRONGER THAN DEATH

The New Testament book of John depicts the Cross as glorious. But what is so glorious about the cross of Christ? It serves as the central symbol of the Christian faith. It stands at the center of our worship. But why did John call it glorious?

In Jesus' time, death by crucifixion was reserved for insurrectionists and the dregs of society. What is so glorious about Jesus experiencing that kind of death?

This question is best answered by considering the larger context of the struggle that occurred between Jesus and the forces that were hostile to God. In Jesus' life, we see success and failure, popularity and enmity, joy and suffering, peace and conflict. Throughout his earthly ministry, Jesus faced opposing forces.

When Jesus was put to death on a cross, it appeared that the opposition had won. It seemed that evil had nailed good to a tree. It witnessed to the failure of Jesus' mission.

However, the Crucifixion is not the end of the story for Christians. Three days later God raised Jesus from the dead. In so doing, God declared that the sacrificial love in Jesus could not be defeated by the power of evil. In raising Jesus, God proclaimed that love is stronger than death and that good had triumphed over evil. The battle was won! The victim had been made the victor.

Celebration takes place on Easter not because of a man who hung on a cross, but because of how God brought victory from what seemed to be defeat. We gather on Easter Sunday to witness to our belief in the resurrection. We gather as an Easter people—people who believe that Christ lives and has not been defeated.

It's worth pondering.

★ PAYING ATTENTION

Paying attention is hard work. I hear the words "Pay attention" often from my wife, my children, my congregants. As a matter of fact, I've heard it all my life!

As a speaker and writer, it is crucial that I pay attention to the ebb and flow of life. Being a keen observer is one of the prerequisites for those of us who comment on life from a Christian perspective.

Observing what happens in the course of a typical day can bring great enjoyment but, more than that, it provides the opportunity to perceive the Holy. Even when life feels fragmentary, fragile, and ambiguous, if I look carefully, I see clues of the Divine.

It is important that we pay attention to those everyday experiences that might contain some hint of the Holy. Pay attention to the unexpected sound of your name on somebody's lips. The good dream. The strange coincidence. The moment that brings tears to your eyes. The person who invigorates your life. Even the smallest events can become holy moments.

Luke's account of the Resurrection includes a visit from the Holy in everyday life. On the day of the Resurrection, two men were walking to a village named Emmaus. As they walked along the road, Jesus himself drew near and went with them. Luke says that the eyes of these two men were kept from recognizing him. The risen Christ appeared to them, but they did not see him.

My word to you during the season of Easter is simple—the risen Christ appears to us each and every day. He is around every corner. He is in the people we meet, the things we see, the experiences that we have. He comes to us again and again.

It is in the everyday experiences that we will meet him—the everyday experiences of praying, listening, and seeing.

It's worth pondering.

⭐ A SEASON OF REDEMPTION

In the secular world, Easter is a day. In the church, Easter is a season that goes from Easter Sunday until Pentecost. Easter is more than the celebration of springtime, more than a secular holiday, more than a reason for family gatherings.

Easter is not about something that we do but what God has done and continues to do. It is about a God who will not be stopped in the process of redeeming the world.

However, if we read the morning papers, it does not look like redemption is taking place; it looks as if pain and destruction are on the rise. Principalities and powers are entrenched. More and more people live under law than under grace. Everything that was once nailed down is coming undone.

The Easter people, however, see life from a different vantage point. People of faith believe that the powers of this world are not as they seem. We believe that in spite of signs to the contrary, God's continuing work of redemption will not be stopped. We believe that the God of the empty tomb cannot be contained.

If we believe that the resurrection of Jesus is true, we must affirm that the God of redemption will win. Ultimately, God will win over evil. Love will win over hate. Right will win over wrong.

Several years ago, the organist of a church I pastored developed a life-threatening illness. Her last trip out of her house was to the organ bench at the church. There on a lonely afternoon, her fingers moved for the last time across the keyboard. With her back as straight as an arrow, and her head tilted back, she played "Christ the Lord Is Risen Today."

If you do not believe that God continues to redeem, tell that to the faithful organist. Convince her and all who also believe. Tell them that God's work was finished with the Cross. Tell them that there is no such thing as the Resurrection.

During the season of Easter, let believers join God in the continuing work of redemption.

It's worth pondering.

 THE MESSAGE OF EASTER

Why do we talk about keeping the spirit of Christmas every day of the year and never say a word about keeping Easter all year long? Should the message of Easter be confined to only one day?

In my opinion, keeping the message of Easter is more important than trying to hold onto the Christmas spirit. I believe this because Christmas is about birth, while Easter is about an eternal love that cannot be defeated by death. Death, as illustrated by the Cross, does not have the last word. When God raised Jesus from the dead to be Christ, God broke the power of death. Easter proclaims that nothing can overcome love.

Thus, the theological notion that Christ lives is of a greater consequence than the time and circumstances of his birth. I believe this to be true because Jesus could have been born and not been raised. If he had not been raised, of what value is his birth?

It's worth pondering.

✦ SINNERS REDEEMED

Lent, more than any time in the church year, brings us face-to-face with our sinfulness. It is difficult for some of us to think of ourselves as sinners. However, Paul boldly said "All have sinned and fall short of the glory of God" (Rom. 3:23). Thus, none of us is spared the taint of sin because all of us have tried to assert our own will against God.

Sin has such a hold on us that we do not have the power to break free by our own actions or through our resolutions or decisions. Sin is always there before us, and it is vast and inescapable. We cannot run away from it or hide from it or deny it.

If we compare ourselves to others, we can feel virtuous, even proud. By comparison, we are no better and no worse than our neighbors. Such comparisons tend to help us deny our sinful natures. However, another comparison is larger and more critical.

During Lent, we compare ourselves not to our neighbors, but to what Christ achieved through his journey to the cross. When we compare ourselves to what was achieved through Christ, all of us are sinners because all of us fall short.

To put the matter rather bluntly: We sin each time we fail to live in the fullness of Christ. If sin is falling short of the image of God that was in Jesus, then all of us are sinners. That, in my judgment, is what Paul meant when he said that "all fall short."

If Lent helps us to see ourselves as sinners, Easter points to how God redeems us from the sin that enslaves us.

It's worth pondering.

★ WHAT ABOUT ELVIS?

I grew up in the same part of town as Elvis Presley. I went to Tread-well High School, and he went to Humes. I was a Methodist, and he belonged to the Assembly of God. I liked debate, and he enjoyed the guitar. We obviously had little in common.

My earliest memory of Elvis took place at a softball field located in North Memphis. While my team was sweating out a ballgame, Elvis was sitting in the bleachers strumming a guitar. No one—except a few girls—paid any attention to Elvis. My teammates made fun of him. Mocked his crooning voice. Dared him to get dirty with the rest of us.

My last memory of Elvis was at Baptist Memorial Hospital in 1976. I was visiting one of my parishioners who happened to be on the same floor. While I was attending to my congregant, a nurse came into the room. I asked if she were the nurse for Elvis. She said she was.

"How is he?" I inquired. With a soft voice she replied, "Not good, not good at all. But have you heard that he gave me a new car?" Point-ing to the keys pinned to her uniform she said, "I carry these with me all of the time and would not let them out of my sight. He let me pick out the car that I wanted. It's a honey."

The decision of the United States Postal Service to create an Elvis Presley commemorative stamp kicked up those youthful memories. Colonel Tom Parker, Elvis's manager, would be proud that his boy from Third Avenue Public Housing Project made it all the way to a stamp.

The real tragedy about Elvis is that he was more an image than a person. The person that I knew was shy. He had a ton of raw tal-ent, which stood ready to be packaged for the mainstream. He came along at a time when Madison Avenue was gearing up to give America a steady diet of new images, products, music, movies, and values. I have often wondered if it was timing that created the Elvis image, or if it was "the King" who pushed his fame toward new vistas. Perhaps it was a combination of both. Nevertheless, Elvis will be remembered as a revi-talizer of rock and roll and a creator of a unique blend of country music and rhythm and blues. No one would dispute that.

Thinking about my sandlot friend and his life causes me to consider my own journey. Am I more image or person?

Lent provides forty days to measure the hidden and revealed places of my life and encourages me to look at myself, not for how I want "my public" to see me but at what I need to see about myself.

Elvis and I *do* have something in common. We are both marked by sin and grace, law and gospel, fear and hope.

No one will ever consider putting me on a stamp. But I know beyond doubt that I have been stamped with the image of God. So have you. So has Elvis.

It's worth pondering.